Osteology Of Haplocanthosaurus, With Description Of A New Species And Remarks On The Probable Habits Of The Sauropoda And The Age And Origin Of The Atlantosaurus Beds: Additional Remarks On Diplodocus, Volume 2

John Bell Hatcher

OSTEOLOGY OF HAPLOCANTHOSAURUS,[1] WITH DESCRIPTION OF A NEW SPECIES, AND REMARKS ON THE PROBABLE HABITS OF THE SAUROPODA AND THE AGE AND ORIGIN OF THE ATLANTOSAURUS BEDS.

By J. B. HATCHER.

The present paper is the third of a series of memoirs based on the fossil vertebrata in the collections of the Carnegie Museum. These memoirs, prepared either directly by the curator of the Department of Vertebrate Paleontology, by his assistants, or others under his general direction, will continue to appear at irregular intervals. Their chief purpose will be to describe in detail and to illustrate with fidelity some of the more important fossil skeletons in the collections. While in every instance these papers will be based on material belonging to the collections of the Carnegie Museum, for the sake of completeness, wherever other and supplementary material is accessible in the collections of other museums it will be utilized and the fullest credit will, in all such instances, be given for such favors. The precarious conditions attending the preservation, fossilization, and final recovery of the skeletons of extinct vertebrates have necessarily been such as to render the occurrence of really complete skeletons conspicuously rare. This is especially true of the gigantic Sauropoda, and notwithstanding the very large collections in several of our leading museums, it is still possible to determine anything like the complete osteology of the different genera only by selecting the best preserved skeleton of each as a basis and supplementing this from material pertaining to the same genus but to other skeletons and belonging to the same or other museums. Owing to the cordial relations at present existing between the various museums of this country, aided by

[1] Proc. Biol. Soc. Wash., Vol. XVI., 1903, pp. 1 and 2, and p. 100.

the exceptional energy with which a few institutions are increasing their collections our knowledge of the structure and relations of a considerable number of known dinosaurian genera has been materially increased during the past few years, while occasional discoveries of entirely new forms have been announced.

It appears somewhat remarkable however that a Sauropod dinosaur of such gigantic size and showing such distinctive generic characters as does *Haplocantho-saurus* should have been discovered so recently at the exact locality, near Canyon City, Colorado, so long worked and rendered classic by the researches of the late Professor Othniel Charles Marsh. This discovery may be taken as an indication not only of the great wealth of this particular locality in the remains of the Dinosauria but of the great diversity that existed in the reptilian life of this region in Jurassic times. For since this single bone quarry, restricted in area to a few hundred square feet and with the bone-bearing horizon not more than three feet thick vertically, has already produced representatives of at least a dozen genera and species and twice or thrice that number of individual skeletons it would seem difficult to overestimate the wealth of the reptilian fauna of this region in Jurassic times or to exaggerate the total number of genera and species that must have existed throughout the period of time required for the deposition of the several hundred feet of sandstones and shales that here constitute that formation and imbedded within which we may still hope to find remains of additional genera and species pertaining to that peculiar but long since extinct group, the Dinosauria.

For the material upon which the present paper is based we are indebted first of all to the generosity of Mr. Andrew Carnegie whose munificence made it possible to carry on the excavations necessary for its recovery. To the skill, energy and patience however of Mr. W. H. Utterback we are directly indebted for its recovery from the hard, almost granitic sandstones in which the bones lay buried beneath many feet of other sandstones and shales only a little less refractory than those actually containing the fossils. After these superincumbent sandstones and shales had been removed over a considerable area the actual and more difficult work of developing and recovering the fossil bones was begun. These, as has been stated above, lay buried in a thick stratum of heavily bedded and hard sandstone. Not only was this sandstone for the most part extremely hard but it was also considerably fractured in such manner as greatly to increase the difficulty encountered in taking up the bones in a proper manner. All difficulties were however met and overcome by Mr. Utterback with commendable patience and ingenuity, and the different blocks were received at the paleontological laboratory of the museum with all the vertebræ and other bones in each block still in their original

positions relative to one another. While aided by diagrams of the quarry, reproduced here in Figs. 1 and 2, and the proper marking of each block as it was taken
up, it is now easily possible to assign the different blocks to their proper position in
the quarry and thus to determine with accuracy the relative positions of all the
different bones as they lay imbedded in the rock.

In the laboratory the bones have been very carefully and skillfully freed from
the matrix under the direction of Mr. Arthur S. Coggeshall as Chief Preparator
assisted by Messrs. W. H. Utterback, L. S. Coggeshall and A. W. VanKirk.

When freed from the matrix the bones were all faithfully drawn by Mr Sydney
Prentice, draughtsman in the Paleontological Department of this Museum.

The type No. 572 of the present genus consists of the two posterior cervicals,
ten dorsals, five sacrals, nineteen caudals, both ilia, ischia and pubes, two chevrons,
a femur and a nearly complete series of ribs, all in an excellent state of preservation
and pertaining to an individual fully adult as is shown by the coössified neural
spines and centra.

POSITION OF THE DIFFERENT BONES AS THEY LAY IMBEDDED IN THE QUARRY.

The pelvis, sacrum, left femur and nineteen anterior caudals were the first portions of the skeleton discovered. They lay in the position shown at A. 572 in the
diagrams of the quarry shown in Figs. 1 and 2. The ilia, ischia and pubes still occupied approximately their normal positions relative to the sacrum, and the femur
was directed backward and downward, with the head removed about two feet from
the acetabulum. The anterior caudal was displaced from its normal position relative to the distal extremity of the sacrum, but the succeeding eighteen caudals were
interlocked by their zygapophyses. The two chevrons lay as shown in the diagram,
approximately in position, with caudals eight and thirteen. I personally assisted
in taking up this portion of the skeleton and am therefore somewhat familiar with
its appearance as it lay in the quarry.

At a distance of about twelve feet but on the same level as the pelvis and bones
above mentioned, were found the nine posterior dorsal vertebræ shown at B. 572 in
the diagrams of the quarry. These were all interlocked by the zygapophyses and most
of the ribs were still in place. The last of this series agrees very well in size and
general appearance with the first sacral of the series found at A. 572, and there would
seem no good reason for assuming that the two series pertain to other than one and
the same skeleton, though, of course, this cannot be absolutely demonstrated, but
the characters exhibited by the two series demonstrate that they pertain to the same
species at least and I have little doubt but that they belong to the same individual.

With the ninth from the posterior of this series of vertebræ there was an interruption, and the three vertebræ shown at C. 572 were found closely adjacent to the an-

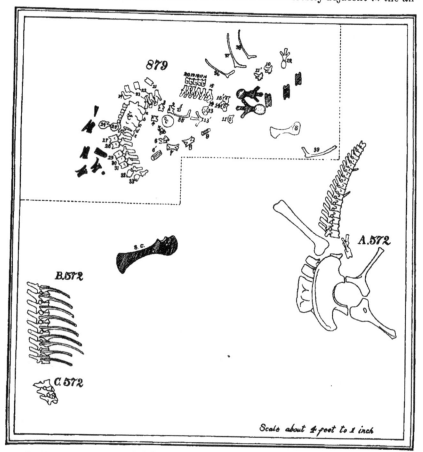

FIG. 1. Diagram of west end of that portion of bone quarry near Canyon City, Colo., worked by W. H. Utterback, showing the positions in which the types of *Haplocanthosaurus priscus* (No. 572, *A*, *B*, *C*) and *H. utterbackii* (No. 879) were found. The shaded bones pertain to a different genus. *A.* 572 femur, pelvis, sacrum and nineteen anterior caudals ; *B.* 572 nine posterior dorsals ; *C.* 572 first dorsal and last two cervicals.

terior of the nine dorsals mentioned. These three vertebræ were interlocked by their zygapophyses and consist of the first dorsal and the last two cervicals. They evidently pertain to the same series as the nine dorsals and the differences in the spines, positions of the rib facets, etc., demonstrate that a number of dorsals are missing between this first dorsal and the anterior of the series of nine posterior dorsals ; while the remains of a second skeleton pertaining to a different species of the same genus fixes the number of missing dorsals at four. This would place the number of free dorsals in the present genus and species at fourteen instead of ten, the probable number in *Diplodocus* and *Morosaurus*. It is possible, however, that in the Dinosauria the number of dorsals may vary in different individuals within the same species as is well known to be the case in numerous instances in the Mammalia.

The bones within the dotted lines in the upper left-hand corner of the first diagram (Fig. 1) for the most part pertain to and constitute the type of a new species of *Haplocanthosaurus*, which will be described later in this paper. The shaded bones

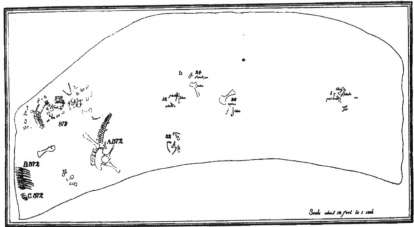

FIG. 2. — Diagram of that portion of bone quarry near Canyon City, Colo., worked by Mr. W. H. Utterback for Carnegie Museum. The lower irregular line shows limit to which quarry had been worked by the late M. P. Felch for Professor Marsh.

within the dotted lines and the scapula and coracoid beneath pertain to one or more genera different from *Haplacanthosaurus*. The relative positions of these bones as they lay imbedded in the sandstones are well shown in the diagrams and will be referred to in detail, when we come to describe the species of which they form the type.

The quarry from which these remains were recovered is the one long worked by Professor Marsh. It is situated on the west side of Oil Creek (Four Mile Creek) at the entrance to Garden Park and some nine or ten miles east by north of Canyon

City, Colorado. The horizon is in the Jurassic[2] and some 100 to 150 feet above the summit of the red Triassic? sandstones It is I believe a decidedly lower horizon than the dinosaur beds near Morrison, Colo.; Como, Little Medicine Bow and Sheep Creeks, Wyoming or Piedmont, South Dakota.

In the diagram of the quarry shown in Fig. 2 the bottom line shows the limit to which the quarry had been worked by Professor Marsh while the area above this line is that worked by Mr. Utterback for the Carnegie Museum.

DESCRIPTION OF THE TYPE (No. 572) OF HAPLOCANTHOSAURUS PRISCUS.

The Vertebræ.

The Cervicals (Plate I., Figs. *C* 15 and 14). —Only the last two cervicals were recovered. Fortunately these, together with the first dorsal, were still interlocked by their zygapophyses and thus the actual position of these three vertebræ in the vertebral column can be definitely determined. They were somewhat crushed and distorted, but considering the hard and fractured nature of the sandstone in which they were imbedded they are in a very good state of preservation and remarkably complete. These vertebræ are rather low, broad and short for the posterior cervicals of a Sauropod dinosaur of such dimensions as is indicated by the remains of the present skeleton and suggest a reptile with a neck which, though, of moderate length, was decidedly more abbreviated than was that of *Diplodocus*, a contemporaneous but more highly specialized Sauropod.

The Fourteenth? Cervical (Plate I., Fig. *C* 14).—Assuming that there were the same number of vertebræ in the cervical series of *Haplocanthosaurus* as in *Diplodocus*, the first of the series of vertebræ now under consideration would correspond to the fourteenth cervical. It is not improbable, however, that the number of cervicals in the present genus was less than in *Diplodocus*. Hence, I have interrogated the numerical position of this vertebra in the cervical series, although as already stated, there can be no doubt of its being the last but one of that series.

The centrum is strongly opisthocœlous and with the transverse diameter exceeding the vertical, though these dimensions have doubtless been somewhat altered by pressure. The sides of the centrum are invaded by long and deep pleurocentral cavities[3] separated only by a thin median septum. These cavities are extended forward into the base of the ball of the centrum while posteriorly they are only separated by a thin plate of bone from the cavity for the ball of the succeeding vertebra.

---

[2] By some considered as Lower Cretaceous.

[3] For an explanation of the names applied to the various cavities, laminæ, etc. of the Sauropod vertebræ, see the author's paper on *Diplodocus*, Mem. Car. Mus., Vol. I., No. 1, pp. 16–19.

In this manner the centrum of the vertebra is reduced to superior and inferior horizontal plates united by a vertical median septum or plate. At the posterior extremity these plates expand into a deeply excavated disk which forms the cup for the succeeding vertebra while at the anterior extremity they unite to form the ball of the centrum. A cross-section of the centrum midway between the anterior and posterior extremities is irregularly I-shaped and somewhat suggestive of that of an I beam in structural materials. The inferior surface of the centrum is broad and flat, much expanded posteriorly and moderately expanded anteriorly where at a point a little back of the ball it gives rise to the cervical rib. The cervical rib is firmly coössified both with the centrum below, through the intermedium of a parapophysis, and with the diapophysis above. There is a short anterior branch of the cervical rib and a longer posterior one. The latter stops short of the posterior extremity of the centrum. It is proportionately broader and stronger than in *Diplodocus carnegii* but decidedly shorter and less robust than in *Brontosaurus excelsus*.

Seen in front this vertebra appears rather low, with broadly expanded cervical ribs and prezygapophyses. There is a single supraprezygapophysial cavity and two infraprezygapophysial cavities separated by a median septum formed by the union of the horizontal laminæ of opposite sides and supported below by the superior wall of the neural canal. In the vertebra under consideration the greater portion of this septum has been lost. It is restored in plaster, and in the drawings the restored parts are indicated by broken lines in the shading. As shown in the drawings the neural spine is also absolutely simple instead of deeply bifurcated as are the spines of the vertebræ of this region in all other known genera of Sauropod dinosaurs wherever it has been possible to determine their character. The neural canal is rather large as compared with that in *Diplodocus*.

Seen from the rear the neural canal is nearly circular and appears as if sunk into the superior surface of the centrum. The postzygapophysial laminæ each send forward a broad thin plate. These unite with the neural spine and enclose a very deep suprapostzygapophysial cavity while below as in front there are two small but deep infrapostzygapophysial cavities separated by a median septum.

The diapophyses are only moderately expanded and they are braced anteroposteriorly by the horizontal laminæ and inferiorly by the inferior branches of the diapophysial laminæ which are very short and almost perpendicular. There is no superior branch of the diapophysial lamina. The posterior branch of the horizontal lamina runs obliquely upward and backward from the diapophysis to the posterior zygapophysis, thus giving additional support to the latter element. Another lamina, horizontal in position but homologous with one of the oblique laminæ, runs directly backward from the diapophysis nearly to the posterior border of the centrum. There are deep and well-defined post-, pre-, supra- and infradiapophysial cavities.

The Fifteenth? or last Cervical (Plate I., Fig. *C* 15). — This vertebra differs from the one preceding it in being a little shorter and with more widely expanded neural spine and cervical ribs. The pleurocentral cavity is less extended posteriorly than in the preceding cervical and its bottom is interrupted by an oblique and an intersecting lamina. There is a shallow infracentral cavity on either side of the median line on the inferior surface near the anterior end of the centrum. There is a single infraprezygapophysial cavity. The neural spine is absolutely simple as in the preceding cervical. The postzygapophyses are higher and the posterior branch of the horizontal lamina consequently more nearly vertical than in the preceding vertebra. The anterior branch of the horizontal lamina has the margin somewhat expanded as shown in Plate I., Fig. *C* 15, indicating that this vertebra gave some support to the scapula.

The First Dorsal (Plate I., Fig. 1). — Fortunately as has already been stated this vertebra and the two preceding were still closely interlocked by their zygapophyses when discovered in the quarry. They were taken up in a single block of the enclosing sandstone and were received at the museum still occupying their original positions relative to one another. In consideration of these facts there can be no question regarding the exact position of these three vertebræ in the vertebral column. That the vertebra now under consideration was a dorsal is conclusively shown not by the presence of tubercular and capitular rib facets showing that it supported on either side a free rib, for there are in our collections of sauropods, skeletons of other dinosaurs fully adult but, with the posterior cervical, bearing free cervical ribs articulating by both tubercular and capitular facets as do the ribs of the dorsal region. The character in this vertebra distinguishing it as a dorsal is the broadly expanded external border of the anterior branch of the horizontal lamina. This element has been thus modified in this and the succeeding dorsal, no doubt, as is known to be the case in *Diplodocus* to give greater surface for the attachment of the powerful muscles necessary for the support of the scapula. That this was the first and not the similarly modified second dorsal is conclusively demonstrated by the fact that it was found interlocked by its zygapophyses with the last cervical.

This vertebra is essentially complete, although the form of the centrum has been considerably altered by crushing. In the accompanying drawings this distortion has been eliminated as much as possible. The length of the centrum is noticeably less than that of the last cervical and the antero-posterior diameter of the pleurocentral cavity is greatly shortened. The floor of this cavity is interrupted by neither oblique nor intersecting laminæ. There is no infracentral cavity. The capitular rib facet is nearly circular and slightly pedunculate. Its position is beneath the anterior border of the pleurocentral cavity.

The neural arch is decidedly higher than in the posterior cervicals. The diapophyses are more widely expanded and support at their extremities small triangular tubercular rib facets which face outward and a little downward. These rib facets are not pendant as they are in this and the two succeeding dorsals in *Diplodocus*. The anterior and posterior zygapophyses are both somewhat more elevated than the diapophyses and they are supported laterally by the anterior and posterior blades of the horizontal laminæ which are subequal and unite at an obtuse angle to form and give support to the transverse process or diapophysis. Throughout about two thirds of its length the external margin of the anterior blade of the horizontal lamina presents a greatly expanded rugose surface, which no doubt served for the muscular attachment of the scapula. From below, the transverse process is supported by the short, rather slender inferior blade or branch of the diapophysial lamina which runs obliquely downward and forward to unite with the superior branch of the prezygapophysial lamina, while an extended and powerful oblique lamina runs obliquely downward and backward, uniting with the lateral wall of the neural arch and giving additional support to the transverse process. The pre-, infra- and postdiapophysial cavities are all deep and well enclosed, while the supradiapophysial cavity is shallow and left open anteriorly.

Seen from in front this vertebra appears low with the transverse processes, zygapophyses and neural spine greatly expanded. The neural spine is low and extremely broad. The apex on one side is injured. It is quite simple, not at all bifurcated and with a broad, rugose, median surface. The anterior aspect of the spine is strongly convex transversely throughout its entire length. The articular surfaces of the anterior zygapophyses are elliptical in outline, with the transverse diameter the greater. Between the anterior zygapophyses there extends a thin lamina having the appearance of a broad shelf or platform. Inferiorly the zygapophyses are supported by the powerful inferior branches of the prezygapophysial laminæ while the superior branches of these laminæ are rudimentary. The infrazygapophysial cavity is deep and simple, the supra- is quite shallow.

Posteriorly there is a deep cup on the centrum for the reception of the ball of the succeeding vertebra. The articular surface of the posterior zygapophysis faces downward and outward.

The postzygapophysial laminæ are branched, the internal and smaller of these branches from the zygapophyses of the opposite sides meet in the middle line and form a widely open V. The supra- and infrapostzygapophysial cavities are very deep and at the bottom the latter is subdivided into three unequal pockets by two short, delicate laminæ. On the posterior surface of the neural spine there is a median rugose surface suggestive perhaps of a postspinal lamina.

As has already been remarked, the series of vertebræ was interrupted at the first dorsal and a number of the succeeding vertebræ are missing from the series. I have estimated the number of missing dorsals at four, the second, third, fourth and fifth. If this estimate is correct, and there are many reasons for believing that it is, as will appear later, the first dorsal of the series of nine mentioned above as pertaining to this skeleton would be the sixth of the dorsal series. That these two series of vertebræ pertained to one and the same skeleton is demonstrated beyond the possibility of a reasonable doubt, not alone by their proximity to one another in the quarry where they lay imbedded in the sandstone as shown in Figs. 1 and 2 at B. 572 and C. 572, but by the relative sizes of the vertebræ, their color and texture and the entirely closed sutures of the neural arches, indicating in each instance an animal of identically the same age.

Figs. 3 and 4 are side views respectively of the supposed sixth and the first dorsal. They are introduced here for direct comparison with one another and to show the great disparity in structure existing between these two vertebræ. These differences become more apparent after an examination of plate A, where posterior and anterior views of the same vertebræ are also given.

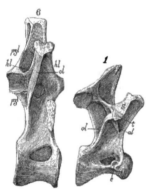

FIG. 3.   FIG. 4.

FIG. 3. Sixth (?) dorsal of type of *Haplocanthosaurus priscus* (No. 572) seen from right side, ⅟₆ natural size, *pzl*, postzygapophysial lamina; *hl*, horizontal lamina; *ol*, oblique lamina.

FIG. 4. First dorsal of same, same view; *ol*, oblique lamina; *al*, inferior blade of diapophysial lamina; *t*, tubercular rib facet; *c*, capitular rib facet; *S*, surface for muscular attachment of scapula, ⅟₆ natural size.

The greatest structural differences exhibited in these two vertebræ are to be found in the relative height of the neural arches, the form and position of the capitular rib facets, the form and positions of the transverse processes and the height and form of the neural spine. All these and many other differences of only less importance will become apparent as we describe the sixth dorsal in detail.

Sixth ? Dorsal (Plate I., Fig. 6).—This vertebra is complete save a small part of the anterior end of the centrum and a portion of the upper part of the neural spine. The entire length of the spine is represented, but the margins, except the posterior, are weathered away and have been restored in plaster. It thus happens that the drawing represents the top of the spine less complete than it actually is.

The centrum was opisthocœlous with the cup moderately deep and the ball at the anterior extremity rather more convex than represented in the drawings It is constricted medially, both laterally and inferiorly, and the inferior surface presents a broad median longitudinal ridge. There are no infracentral cavities. The pleurocentral cavities are large, irregularly triangular in outline and very deep, with the dividing median septum reduced to a thin lamina.

The neural arch is high, much constricted transversely and much shorter anteroposteriorly than the centrum. On the anterior lateral margin of either side it supports an elongated, sessile, capitular rib facet situated midway between the anterior zygapophyses and the superior border of the centrum. This facet is quite unlike that of the succeeding dorsals, it is very distinctive and is most like that of the sixth dorsal in *H. utterbackii* to be described later, as compare Plates I. and II.

The transverse processes are high and directed obliquely upward and outward at an angle of about forty-five degrees. At their extremities they bear tubercular rib facets which face outward and a little upward. Inferiorly the transverse process is supported by a powerful lamina arising from the posteroexternal border of the neural arch and forming the greater portion of the broad posterior surface of the transverse process. Although this lamina occupies a position identical with that of the inferior blade of the *diapophysial lamina* in the corresponding dorsal of *Diplodocus*, nevertheless it is clearly homologous with the *oblique lamina* of the first dorsal of this skeleton. In this vertebra the *diapophysial lamina*, only the inferior branch of which is represented in the last cervical and first dorsal described above, has become quite obsolete. There is, in *Haplocanthosaurus*, no division of the anterior blade of the horizontal lamina into superior and inferior branches such as has been shown to be the case in the anterior dorsals of *Diplodocus carnegii*. This fact at once distinguishes that lamina marked *al* and *dl*, in the first dorsal and last cervical as the diapophysial and that marked *ol*, as an oblique lamina, though in no sense to be considered as homologous with the oblique lamina that in the middorsals of *Diplodocus carnegii* gives support posteriorly and inferiorly to the capitular rib facet.

The anterior blade of the horizontal lamina is long and broad, the posterior short and narrow. There is a short and narrow superior blade of the diapophysial lamina invading the bottom of the deep supradiapophysial cavity shown at *dl*, in

Plate I., Fig. 6, second column, and a little anterior to this is a second lamina *al*, which may be an anterior branch of the superior blade of the diapophysial lamina, but which is interpreted as a branch of the prespinal.

Although the transverse process appears massive it is really very light and thin, and save toward the base it is made up entirely of the anterior blade of the horizontal lamina and the oblique lamina. These two laminæ meet at nearly right angles so as to enclose a very deep trough which opens downward, forward and outward and is confluent with the very deep infradiapophysial cavity. There is no prediapophysial cavity and the postdiapophysial cavity is very shallow and inconspicuous.

Seen from in front, the neural arch appears high and constricted just beneath the capitular rib facets but expanded in the region of the superior border of those surfaces. The anterior zygapophyses are elevated and have the articular surfaces elongated transversely and abbreviated antero-posteriorly. Beneath the anterior zygapophyses there is a deep infraprezygapophysial cavity confluent with a deep trough into which the neural canal opens. The supraprezygapophysial cavity is shallow and separated from the one below by a short, stout, transverse plate which gives support superiorly to the lateral borders of the neural arch. In cross-section the neural spine is triangular with the apex of the triangle directed forward and forming the rather broad and rugose prespinal surface.

Seen from behind, the neural spine is broad and rugose, though much narrower than in the first dorsal. This is due to the greater development of the superior blades of the postzygapophysial laminæ, which are thin and expanded and continue to the summit of the neural spine. There are shallow supra- and infrazygapophysial cavities and the latter is much elongated and inclosed laterally by the inferior blades of the postzygapophysial laminæ. These give support inferiorly to a well-formed hyposphenal process developed on this and the succeeding dorsals showing that in addition to the ordinary zygapophysial articulation of the preceding vertebræ the dorsals of this region had a hyposphene-hypantrum articulation.

Dorsals Seven? to Fourteen? Inclusive (Plate I., Figs. 7–14). — After the above rather tedious detailed description of the posterior cervicals and dorsals one and six?, the succeeding dorsals may best be described together. Since, in their more important and general characters, they agree very well both with one another and with the supposed sixth dorsal just described, the following description may very well be limited to a general reference to those characters wherein they all agree, followed by a special reference to the more important distinctive characters of each, wherever such exist. As already stated, these vertebræ, together with the one last described when discovered in the quarry near Canyon City, Colorado, were all closely interlocked by their zygapophyses. They were taken up in a single block of matrix and were received at the museum still imbedded in the sandstone and in their exact original position relative to one another. Thus whatever question there may be regarding their position relative to the last cervical, there can be absolutely no question regarding their position relative to each other, while the same can be said with only a little less certainty regarding their position in relation to the sacrum, for the supposed fourteenth or last of this series, although removed some ten feet from the sacrum, agrees very well in size with the first sacral and has the posterior extremity modified for articulation with that vertebra. There can be no reasonable doubt but that these dorsals and cervicals formed part of the same skeleton as that to which belonged the pelvis and caudals shown in Plates III., IV., V., and the femur shown in text Fig. 14.

In the dorsals now under consideration, the centra are comparatively small, constricted medially, opisthocœlous throughout, though less decidedly so in the posterior region. They are subequal in length, with those of the posterior region a little shorter than those of the anterior. The pleurocentral cavities are deep and subequal in area. They are all irregularly ovate in outline with the broader end directed anteriorly. The neural arches are high and the neural spines short and stout. There is a striking contrast in the proportionate length of the neural spines and height of the neural arches in the dorsals of *Haplocanthosaurus* when compared with those elements in the same vertebræ of any other genus of Sauropod dinosaur known to the present writer. This contrast is especially noticeable in *Diplodocus and Brontosaurus* but is less marked in *Morosaurus*. The capitular facets are somewhat pedunculate and gradually assume a more elevated position in the anterior dorsals until the eighth is reached when they attain an elevation equal to that of the anterior zygapophyses. In the eighth and succeeding dorsals their position remains constant. The transverse processes throughout the entire series of vertebræ now under consideration are subequal in length and are directed upward and outward at an angle of about forty-five degrees. The transverse processes of the posterior dorsals are somewhat more slender than are those of the anterior dorsals. Commencing with the eighth dorsal the superior blade of the diapophysial lamina becomes very well developed and in this and the succeeding vertebræ it unites, about midway up the spine, with the superior blade of the postzygapophysial lamina to form a single lamina giving lateral support to the neural spine. The posterior position of the extremity of the transverse process in the eighth dorsal as shown in Plate I., Fig. 8, is due to distortion and is not the normal position of that element. In the seventh and succeeding dorsals the antero-posterior diameter of the neural spines exceeds the transverse and the extremities of all these vertebræ are somewhat expanded and rugose. All the dorsals of this region exhibit the hyposphene-hypantrum articulation.

The Sacrum (Plates IV. and V.). — In the present skeleton as in all other fully adult Sauropod dinosaurs to whatsoever known genus or species they may pertain, there are five vertebræ, coössified by their centra and functioning as sacrals by giving support to the ilia either by means of so-called sacral ribs or transverse processes or by both these elements. Whether or not all five of these vertebræ should be regarded as true sacrals must remain very largely a matter of individual opinion. This matter has already been discussed at some length by the present writer in his paper on *Diplodocus* which formed the first of a series of memoirs, which will continue to appear from time to time relating to the dinosaur remains in the collections of this museum.

Whether the number of true sacrals in the Sauropoda be five or less it is evident that in those genera of American Sauropods where the complete sacrum is known, namely, *Diplodocus, Brontosaurus, Morosaurus* and *Haplocanthosaurus,* the number of vertebræ functioning as sacrals, that is giving support to the ilia, is constant and is in no sense different in or diagnostic of the several genera as was supposed by the late Professor Marsh. It frequently happens in the case of isolated sacra pertaining to young individuals that one or two of the functional sacrals through not having been firmly coössified with the three vertebræ which, according to the present writer's opinion, constitute the true sacrals, have become detached and lost and in this manner the number of functional sacrals has been mistakenly reduced to either three or four according as the number of detached vertebræ was one or two. By an unfortunate circumstance this proved to be the case with the sacra of *Diplodocus* and *Morosaurus* first discovered and described by Marsh. The sacrum of the first of these genera was found detached and consisted of three coössified centra, while in that of the second (the type of *M. grandis*) there were four coössified centra. From these circumstances Professor Marsh quite naturally concluded that the number of functional sacrals in these genera was respectively three for the former and four for the latter and proceeded to make those numbers diagnostic of the genera and families to which they pertained. Subsequent discovery of more complete material has demonstrated beyond a doubt the number of functional sacrals to be five in each of these genera as in *Brontosaurus.* The fragmentary sacra of *Apatosaurus* and *Atlantosaurus* figured by Marsh are evidently incapable of furnishing any definite proof as to the exact number of sacrals in those genera, which should they finally prove to be valid will doubtless also be found to be provided with five functional sacrals. The same remark also applies to the recently described genus *Brachiosaurus* of Riggs. On the other hand it sometimes happens in the skeletons of very old individuals that an anterior caudal or posterior dorsal becomes coössified with the functional sacrals. As an example of the latter the sacrum of the type of *Brontosaurus excelsus* Marsh may be cited. In such instances however there is no danger of misinterpreting the additional vertebræ since they never bear so-called sacral ribs ribs or give any support to the ilia.

The sacrum in the present genus and species may be described in general as being broad, low, with short neural spines and consisting of five vertebræ with subequal, coössified centra. All five of these vertebræ bear parapophyses (sacral ribs) and give support to the ilia through the intermedium of these and the diapophyses. The parapophyses of the three median or true sacrals expand distally and unite to form the inner superior border of the acetabulum as is well shown in Plate V., Fig. 1.

Seen from below (Plate V., Fig. 1) the sacral centra appear subequal in length with the transverse diameter of the first and last exceeding that of either of the three median or true sacrals. All five of these vertebræ bear so-called sacral ribs springing directly from the middle of the centra, save that of the first, which springs from the superior internal border of the centrum. The excellent state of preservation in which this sacrum was found, firmly attached to the ilia of either side, demonstrates beyond a doubt the fact that all five of the vertebræ bear those processes which have been called sacral ribs. As to whether or not the first of the sacrals is homologous with that which in *Diplodocus* I have described as the last dorsal, though there functioning as a sacral, I am as yet undecided. I believe, however, that it is, although since it is the neural spines of this and the two succeeding vertebræ that are coössified in the present sacrum, this fact might be considered by some as tending to disprove this assumption, for in *Diplodocus* it is the spines of the three median vertebræ, *the true sacrals*, that are coössified. However this may be, I am inclined to the opinion that the first vertebra which in *Diplodocus* gives support to the ilia did in fact bear what has usually been interpreted as a sacral rib and should therefore be considered as a sacral by those who accept the presence of this element as distinguishing the sacrals. The imperfect condition of all the *Diplodocus* sacra so far discovered precludes the possibility of determining this point with absolute certainty in that genus. In the type of *Diplodocus carnegii* the right side of this vertebra is present though in a somewhat imperfect condition and presents an element which, though occupying a decidedly more elevated position than that of the so-called sacral ribs in the succeeding sacrals, does however spring from the superior lateral surface of the centrum. It may therefore be considered as homologous with those elements in the true sacrals. Its position with relation to the vertebral centrum may be considered as evidence that this vertebra though functioning as a sacral is in reality a modified dorsal and that, contrary to Osborn's assertion, the sacrum in the Sauropoda may have expanded by the addition of at least one posterior dorsal.

The diapophyses of all the sacral vertebræ send downward thin vertical diapophysial laminæ. These unite at their extremity with the sacral ribs or as I prefer to call them the parapophyses[4] of their respective vertebræ to form thin partitions separating the four large sacral foramina to be seen in the inferior view of this sacrum with ilia attached, shown in Fig. 1, Plate V. Internally these foramina are enclosed by the sacral centra and externally by the extended iliac bar formed by the expanded and coalesced distal extremities of the parapophyses (sacral ribs).

The parapophyses (sacral ribs) of the first and fifth sacrals are longer but rather more slender than those of the three median or true sacrals. This is especially true of the first sacral. In this vertebra this element springs from the superoanterior surface of the centrum, continues outward for some distance as a strong bar when it expands and divides into two branches enclosing a small foramen bounded externally by the ilium and shown in Plate V., Fig. 1. The inferior of these two branches abuts against the base of the pubic peduncle, the superior unites with the diapophysial lamina in giving support to the widely expanded anterior blade of the ilium.

In the posterior sacral the parapophysis springs from the middle of the centrum at its anterior extremity and continues as a single bar, only moderately expanded distally, where it gives support to the posterior blade of the ilium. Superiorly it is united throughout its entire length with the diapophysial lamina. The diapophysis branches distally and with the posterior blade of the ilium encloses the foramen seen in Plate V., Fig. 3.

The parapophyses of the three median sacrals are all short and stout. They differ from those of the first and fifth sacrals in having their extremities expanded and coalesced so as to form a strong iliac bar not only giving support to the ilia but constituting the inner superior borders of the acetabula. These three vertebræ were the first to become coössified. Throughout the entire life of the individual they gave the chief, and during a certain period of its youth perhaps, almost the only support to the ilia. It is for these reasons that I consider these vertebræ as the only true sacrals of which the sacrum in the earliest Sauropods was alone composed.

[4] The homologies of these elements will be discussed more fully when we come to speak of the caudals.

Should we ever be so fortunate as to discover representatives of the very earliest Sauropod Dinosaurs it is not at all improbable that in these the sacrum will be found to consist of only these three vertebræ. This number is, however, a decided advance over that which is supposed to have constituted the sacrum in the primitive reptilia. This supposition, however, is at present purely conjectural though supported by considerable evidence. If we consider the three median vertebræ as the *true sacrals* the anterior might very appropriately be called a *dorso-sacral* and the posterior a *sacro-caudal*.

In all the functional sacrals the parapophyses spring from the anterior extremities of the centra of the several vertebræ, but in the first and second *true sacrals* there is in each instance some slight union between the posterior extremities of the centra of these vertebræ and the succeeding parapophysis as shown in Plate V., Fig. 1.

Viewed from above, the diapophyses of the sacrals in *Haplocanthosaurus* are each seen to be formed by the union of two laminæ. One of these springs from the spine of that vertebra to which the process pertains and the other from the antero-external margin of the spine of the immediately posterior sacral. These laminæ rapidly converge both inferiorly and exteriorly and unite in forming the diapophyses or transverse processes. These are on a level with the superior border of the ilium and a short distance before coming in contact with that element they expand anteroposteriorly and present broad, rugose, superior surfaces.

The neural spines of all the sacrals are extremely short as compared with the same elements in either *Diplodocus* or *Brontosaurus* and in this respect they more nearly resemble the same elements in *Morosaurus*. Those of the three posterior sacrals are directed upward and a little backward. The spines of the three anterior sacrals are coalesced and form an elongated bony plate. In *Diplodocus* and *Brontosaurus* it is the three (sometimes the two anterior in the former genus) true median sacrals that have the spines coalesced. Superiorly and posteriorly the spines are much expanded and they each present prominent lateral rugosities at the apex.

Seen from behind or in front the sacrum is considerably distorted by pressure. In the drawings, Plate V., this distortion has been for the most part eliminated and the sacrum appears low and very broad with the neural arches of only moderate height when compared with those of the dorsals. In so far as I have been able to determine there is in the present genus no unusual development of the neural canal in the region of the sacrum.

The principal characters of the sacrum in the present genus are well shown in Plates IV. and V., where in the former comparative views are given of the pelves of *Brontosaurus*, *Diplodocus* and *Haplocanthosaurus* with their respective sacra in position.

The more important dimensions of the sacrum of the type of *Haplocanthosaurus priscus* are as follows:

mm.

Total length of the five coössified sacrals	795
Greatest expanse of transverse processes of first sacral	640
"　　　"　　　"　　　" last "	700
Height of top of neural spine above bottom of centrum in first sacral	520
"　　"　　"　　"　　"　　"　　" last "	485
Anteroposterior length of three coössified neural spines	398
Height of anterior neural spine above zygapophyses	252
"　posterior "　"　"　"	180

The Caudal Vertebræ (Plate III.).—Nineteen anterior caudals were found associated with the present skeleton. Their position in the quarry relative to one another and to the sacrum are shown in Figs. 1 and 2.

The centra throughout the entire series of nineteen caudals are remarkably short when compared with the same vertebræ in *Diplodocus*. They are somewhat constricted medially and are slightly amphicœlous with the concavity of the anterior extremity more pronounced than that of the posterior. The centrum of the first caudal is the shortest of the series. From this they very gradually and slowly increase in length until the twelfth caudal is reached when they begin very gradually to decrease in length.

The neural spines throughout are comparatively short and directed somewhat backward. They are compressed and with rugose extremities which are quite simple throughout instead of being laterally expanded and emarginate as in caudals one to eight in *Diplodocus carnegii*.

The anterior zygapophyses are slender and extended far forward in advance of the anterior extremities of their respective centra. The posterior zygapophyses are not extended beyond the posterior extremities of the centra.

The transverse processes even in the anterior caudals are quite simple when compared with the same elements in *Diplodocus* and *Brontosaurus*. In the anterior caudals they appear as simple, broad plates of bone springing directly from the neural arches and the superior lateral surfaces of the centra. These bony plates are nearly flat and thin. They are entire instead of being perforated as in *Diplodocus*, and their posterior and anterior surfaces are entirely destitute of that series of vertical or radiating laminæ seen in the anterior caudals of *Diplodocus carnegii*. The transverse processes of the caudals decrease rapidly in size as we proceed posteriorly and in the twelfth caudal they are reduced to a rounded knob of bone on either side of the centrum near the superior border, while just above this on the middle of the side of the neural arch there is a second prominence less pronounced, however, than that on the centrum. In the thirteenth caudal the prominence on the centrum is only faintly distinguishable. In the succeeding vertebræ it has disappeared entirely, while that on the neural arch continues on the thirteenth, fourteenth and fifteenth caudals, but is wanting on the succeeding vertebræ. Of these prominences or tuberosities the superior or that one situated on the neural arch doubtless represents a rudimentary *diapophysis*, while the inferior or that situated on the side of the centrum may be considered as homologous with the *parapophysis*. It would, therefore, appear as though the transverse processes in the anterior caudals were made up of the coalesced diapophyses and parapophyses. Just what bearing this may have on the exact homologies of the so-called sacral ribs in the Sauropoda it is impossible to say. It would appear, however, that Osborn's assertion that a "sacral rib is not a transverse process"[5] is open to criticism when that term is applied to these elements in the dinosaur pelvis, or at least needs some further support, and that Marsh's statement that "each sacral vertebra supports its own sacral rib or transverse process" may not have been so far from correct as Osborn supposed it to be, though Marsh's assertion that the sacral vertebræ in the Sauropoda were without diapophyses is doubtless erroneous. If, as Osborn asserts : "The sacrum of Sauropoda (Cetiosaurs) is reinforced by the addition, not of dorsals, but of anterior caudals," it would seem quite evident that those elements which spring from the sacrals and give support to the ilia are in reality only the modified transverse processes of the caudals, and since, as has already been shown, the latter appear to have been formed by the union of parapophyses and diapophyses, there would seem very good reasons for assuming that the so-called sacral ribs which spring directly from the sacral centra are homologous with the parapophyses, while the superior bar giving support to the superior border of the ilium represents the diapophyses and that these two elements with the connecting diapophysial lamina together constitute the transverse process. According to this interpretation the so-called *sacral ribs* become morphologically quite distinct from those elements in the tailed Amphibians as described by Flower on page 66 of his "Osteology of the Mammalia," and I am inclined to the opinion that, while the articulation of the ilium with the sacrum in the Hell Bender (*Menopoma*) and other allied forms is by means of a sacral rib interposed between the ilium and the transverse process of the sacral vertebra in the Sauropoda as well as in all the other terrestrial vertebrates requiring more or less rigidity in this region this interposed sacral rib, if it ever existed, has disappeared altogether, allowing the ilium to come in direct contact with the transverse processes of the sacrum. In *Menopoma* the transverse proc-

[5] See Memoirs Am. Mus. Nat. Hist., Vol. I., Part V., p. 202.

ess of the sacral is stronger not only than those of the preceding and succeeding vertebræ, but it is stronger than its sacral rib, although the latter is more robust than the movable ribs borne by the transverse processes of the immediately preceding and succeeding vertebræ. It would seem more probable, therefore, that the smaller and more slender sacral rib would become obsolete than the stronger and more robust transverse process. Whether this elimination was accomplished by the complete disappearance of the sacral rib or by its fusion with the transverse process cannot be told. It by the latter process, however, the so-called sacral ribs in the Sauropod sacrum would then be homologous with the coalesced sacral ribs and transverse processes. But in the sacra of the Sauropoda and other highly specialized terrestrial vertebrates, whether reptiles or mammals, it would appear to be quite evident that in all those sacral vertebræ added to the primitive sacrum through the modification of anterior caudals it is the *transverse processes* (united diapophyses and paropophyses) that have been modified to give support to the ilia instead of true *sacral ribs* homologous with the free ribs borne at the extremities of the transverse processes in the anterior caudals of *Menopoma*, for in no instance are the transverse processes of the anterior caudals of even moderately specialized terrestrial vertebrates known to have borne such ribs. Even in the modern Iguana and in the crocodiles where the sacrum is still exceedingly primitive consisting of only two ununited vertebræ there are no movable or other ribs on the transverse processes of the anterior caudals and none are known to the present writer even among the earliest known Dinosauria. It does not seem at all reasonable to suppose that these ribs were present in the primitive forms in the caudal region, that they disappeared and then reappeared in the successive caudals as these were added to the primitive sacrum more especially since their presence would tend to produce instability rather than strength in that region where rigidity is especially advantageous. In Figs. 5 and 6 are given superior views of the sacra together with the immediately preceding and succeeding vertebræ in *Menopoma allegheniensis* and *Iguana tuberculata*. A study of these figures shows the marked difference in the structure of the sacrum in the two. In *Menopoma* the ilia articulate with the transverse processes of the solitary sacral through the intermedium of sacral ribs, while in the Iguana this articulation is directly with processes firmly fixed one on either side of the centra of each of the two sacrals. Whatever the exact homologies of these latter processes may be it is impossible to say with certainty, though embryology ought to offer some evidence. In general form and in position, however, it is evident that they approximate much more closely the transverse processes than true sacral ribs. If, however, they are homologous with the true sacral ribs as seen in *Menopoma*, which to the writer seems extremely improbable, it does not follow that they are "profoundly different from the dorsal ribs" as has been stated by Osborn;[5] for an examination of a skeleton of *Menopoma* will show the morphological identity of the sacral ribs with the free ribs borne at the extremities of the transverse processes alike of the anterior caudals and the entire presacral series, while the latter must be homologous with the dorsal ribs

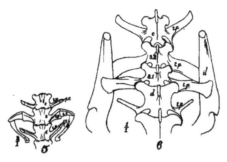

FIG. 5. Superior view of sacral, anterior caudal and posterior dorsal or lumbar of *Menopoma alleghen-iensis*, twice natural size. *s*, sacral; *c*, anterior caudal; *d*, posterior dorsal; *t.p.*, transverse process; *s.r.*, sacral rib; *il*, ilium; *f.r.*, free rib.

FIG. 6. Superior view of sacrum, anterior caudal and posterior lumbar or dorsal of *Iguana tuber-culata*, natural size. *d*, posterior dorsal; *s.1*, first sacral; *s.2*, last sacral; *c*, anterior caudal; *t.p.*, transverse process except that on last dorsal which is a free rib; *il*, ilium.

in the terrestrial vertebrates as will become apparent by a study of the skeleton of *Iguana* where the transition from the short straight ribs of the dorso-lumbar region to the elongated and curved ribs of the true dorsals is quite gradual.

In consideration of the characters just described as obtaining in the transverse processes of the caudals of *Haplocanthosaurus* in connection with those already mentioned as pertaining to the sacrum in the various genera of the Sauropoda, it appears to the present writer that the following characters relative to the structure of the Sauropod sacrum as a whole and the homologies of the different elements with those of the other vertebræ seem quite probable though not at present capable of being demonstrated with certainty.

FIRST. — *That the Sauropod sacrum is composed of five coössified vertebræ which function as sacrals.*

SECOND. — *That the three median of these five functional sacrals alone composed the sacrum in the primitive Sauropoda and may be regarded as the true sacrals.*

[5] Vol. I., Part V., Mem. Am. Mus. Nat. Hist., p. 201.

THIRD. — *That the number of sacrals in the Sauropoda has been increased to five by the addition of a posterior dorsal and an anterior caudal.*

FOURTH. — *That the sacrals give support to the ilia solely by means of the transverse processes (diapophyses and parapophyses).*

FIFTH. — *That there are no true sacral ribs homologous with those elements in the tailed amphibia and that the so-called sacral ribs are really homologous with the parapophyses or inferior branches of the transverse processes.*

It is true that the parapophyses (sacral ribs) of the sacrals, as also the transverse processes of the caudals in the Sauropoda are derived from centers of ossification distinct from those which give origin to the centra, and this fact may by some authorities be taken as proof that they are not portions of the transverse processes, though I should not consider it as such.

The principal dimensions sometimes materially modified by crushing of the several vertebræ in the type of *Haplocanthosaurus priscus* (No. 572) are given in the following table: In column 1 the greatest expanse of the transverse processes of the diapophyses are given; column 2, greatest length of centra; column 3, transverse diameter of centra at posterior extremity; column 4, height of neural spines

	1. mm.	1. in.	2. mm.	2. in.	3. mm.	3. in.	4. mm.	4. in.
? 14. Cervical.			259	11⅜	160	6¼	320	12⅝
? 15. "			247	9¾	150	5⅞	352	13⅞
1. Dorsal.	428	16⅞	224	8¾	153	6	355	14
6. "	420	16½	185	7¼	135	5¼	568	22 5/16
7. "	458	18	173	6¾	145	5⅝	590	23¼
8. "	457	18	165	6½	150	5⅞	551	21⅝
9. "	457	18	185	7¼	154	6	583	22¾
10. "	440	17¼	164	6⅜	153	6	582	22⅞
11. "	430	16⅞	170	6⅝	161	6⅜	597	23½
12. "	425	16¾	150	5⅞	178	7	607	23⅞
13. "	410	16⅛	146	5¾	191	7½	610	24
14. "	410	16⅛	125	4⅞	203	8	615	24¼
1. Caudal.	416	16⅜	103	4	195	7⅝	510	20
2. "	390	15¼	82	3¼	178	7	471	18½
3. "	320	12½	91	3⅝	190	7½	365	14⅜
4. "	353	13⅞	86	3⅜	165	6½	375	14¾
5. "	314	12⅜	94	3⅞	175	6⅞	396	15⅝
6. "	230	9⅛	95	3⅞	137	5⅜	404	15⅞
7. "	?	?	105	4⅛	?	?	415	16⅜
8. "	216	8½	97	—3⅞	125	4 15/16	397	15⅝
9. "			100	4	115	4½	?	?
10. "			114	4½	165	6½	345	13½
11. "			105	4⅛	105	4⅛	338	13¼
12. "			110	4⅜	110	4⅜	314	12⅜
13. "			101	4	114	4½	298	11¾
14. "			100	—4	109	4¼	261	10¼
15. "			100	3⅞	107	4¼	268	10½
16. "			99	4	101	4	261	10¼
17. "			95	3¾	100	+3⅞	237	9⅜
18. "			92	3⅝	100	—4	229	9
19. "			91	3⅝	92	3⅝	210	8¼

above middle of inferior border of centra in presacrals and above inferior border of posterior end in postsacrals.

The inconsistencies that appear in the above table of measurements are due to the varying amount of crushing to which the different vertebræ were subjected while entombed in the sandstones. In this connection it should be remembered that these animals lived in a period long previous to that which witnessed the final upheaval of the front range of the Rocky Mountains and that the bones, as well as the sandstones in which they were imbedded, have been subjected to the enormous pressure which effected the upheaval of that mountain range. Little wonder that they are in many instances much crushed and distorted. It thus happens that the measurements given above are of value only as giving a general idea as to the several dimensions of the various vertebræ. In most instances they cannot be considered as representative of the exact measurements and therefore capable of being compared critically with those of other skeletons.

The Chevrons (Figs. 7, 8, 9, 10). — Only two chevrons were found. One of these (Figs. 7 and 8) was found in position between the eighth and ninth caudals. It does not differ materially from the chevron of the same region in *Diplodocus* or *Brontosaurus*. It is Y-shaped with the open portion somewhat abbreviated and the inferior portion elongated, compressed and with spatulate extremity. The articular surfaces of opposite sides at the proximal ends are not confluent. The length of this chevron is 313 mm. When seen from the side, it curves less strongly backward at the distal end than does the same chevron in *Diplodocus*.

FIGS. 7 and 8, chevron between caudals 8 and 9, side and posterior views respectively, one-tenth natural size.

FIGS. 9 and 10, chevron between caudals 13 and 14, side and posterior views respectively, one-tenth natural size.

The other chevron (Figs. 9 and 10) was found in position articulating with caudals thirteen and fourteen. It differs from the one just described in its smaller size and in the more elongated open portion of the Y as compared with the closed inferior portion. At the point where the two branches meet it is greatly constricted antero-posteriorly, while distally it is much expanded in the same direction, but without the anterior and posterior projections which are already quite prominent in the same and the preceding chevron in *Diplodocus*. This chevron has a length of 184 mm.

The Ribs (Figs. 11, 12 and 13). — The ribs do not differ essentially from those of other members of the Sauropoda. They increase in length and strength quite rapidly from the first to the fourth when they continue subequal in length until in about the region of the ninth or tenth. Posterior to these, they rapidly become shorter and more slender. The ribs of the anterior and mid-dorsal region are much expanded proximally where they present a rather deep concavity on the posterior surface, while the anterior surface in the same region is convex. Beyond this they become subcircular in cross-section and somewhat spatulate at their distal extremities. The ribs of the posterior region are decidedly less expanded proximally and in the middle they are semicircular in cross-section.

Figs. 11, 12 and 13 represent respectively anterior views of the supposed second, fourth and thirteenth ribs. The second rib has a length of 911 mm., the

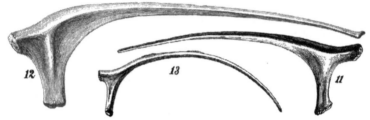

Fig. 11. Anterior view of second? rib of right side, one-tenth nat. size.
Fig. 12. Anterior view of fourth? rib of left side, one-tenth nat. size.
Fig. 13. Anterior view of thirteenth? rib of left side, one-tenth nat. size.

fourth 1,394 mm. and the thirteenth 710 mm. Compared with the size of the animal as a whole the ribs of *Haplocanthosaurus* are neither long nor robust. Throughout the entire series the capitulum and tuberculum are well separated. The capitulum is pediceled while the tuberculum is sessile, save in the anterior ribs where it is also pediceled.

The Pelvis (Plates IV. and V.).

All the elements of the pelvis were found approximately in position and in a splendid state of preservation.

The Ilium (Plate IV., Fig. 3).—In general form the ilium resembles that of other members of the Sauropoda. In the present skeleton both ilia were found attached to the sacrum which lay imbedded in the sandstones with the spines directed upwards but reclining a little on its right side. It thus happened that these elements received the pressure of the superincumbent rocks in a direction obliquely vertical and from the left. This pressure was sufficient to accomplish considerable crushing and the superior borders of the ilia have been considerably flattened and instead of describing the arc of a circle as was doubtless the case before this distortion took place, for a considerable distance along their superior borders they now present a nearly flat surface. In the drawings this distortion has not been entirely eliminated.

The ischiac peduncle is broad and sessile with the transverse diameter of the articular surface for the ischium considerably exceeding the anteroposterior diameter.

The pubic peduncle is elongate, extending far below the inferior border of the ilium. It forms most of the anterior border of the acetabulum. The articular surface for the pubis has the transverse diameter greater than the anteroposterior. At its base the pubic peduncle is supported internally by the parapophyses of the dorso-sacral and the first true sacral vertebra as shown in Plate V., Fig. 11.

The ilium is produced far in front of the pubic peduncle into a broad anterior blade. At its extremity this anterior blade of the ilium is broad instead of pointed as in *Diplodocus* and *Brontosaurus*. In superficial area the anterior blade of the ilium constitutes nearly one half of that element. Internally it is supported by the powerful and widely expanded diapophysis of the dorso-sacral.

The ilia are not produced far behind the ischiac peduncles and the posterior blades are therefore short but rather broad.

The upper one-half of the acetabular border is formed by the ilium, the pubic and ischiac peduncles and the acetabular bar formed by the united extremities of the parapophyses of the three true sacrals.

The anterior extremities of the ilia of opposite sides are very widely separated and the posterior extremities less decidedly so while in the middle, both superiorly and inferiorly the ilia of opposite sides approach more nearly to each other. It thus happens that the diapophyses and parapophyses of the three true sacrals are shorter than those of the dorso-sacral and sacro-caudal.

The Pubis (Plate IV., Fig. 3, and Plate V., Fig. 2).—The pubis is proportionately short and stout and greatly expanded proximally. At their distal extremities the internal borders of the pubes were in contact for a short distance only. Above this point of contact, when in position, the pubes were separated by an elongated aperture 300 millimeters in length, while above this aperture they meet again and form an elongated pubic symphysis about 300 millimeters in length. In either instance the union between the pubes of opposite sides was ligamentary. The direction and position of the superior of the two pubic symphysial surfaces is horizontal and ventral rather than vertical. The pubis forms the antero-inferior one fourth of the acetabulum. The pubic foramen is very large and somewhat elliptical in outline ; just posterior to and above it there is an extended sutural surface for contact with the ischium.

The Ischium (Plate IV., Fig. 3, and Plate V., Fig. 3).—As compared with the pubes the ischia were slender. Proximally they expand and form the postero-inferior one fourth of the acetabular border. Beneath the acetabular border they present broad, rugose, sutural surfaces for articulation with the pubes. Posteriorly the ischia contract rapidly and form broad flat bars with broadly rounded external surfaces. These bars converge and meet distally where they are coössified to form a symphysis about 195 millimeters in length.

The form and principal characters of the different elements of the pelvis are well shown in the figures in the plates accompanying this memoir.

The principal measurements of the different elements of the pelvis are as follows:

	mm.
Greatest length of ilium	827
Distance from inferior extremity of pubic peduncle to top of iliac crest	512
" " " " ischiac " " " "	332
Length of pubic peduncle below superior border of acetabulum	249
Expanse of ilia at anterior extremity	1140
" " " " posterior "	810
" " pubic peduncles	786
" " ischiac "	685
Length of pubis	693
Greatest breadth of pubis	432
Least " " "	165
Length of ischia from middle of acetabular border to distal end	790
Extent of acetabular border of ischium	210
Breadth of ischium just above symphysis	85
Depth " " " " "	50

The Femur (Fig. 14).

Unfortunately the femur is the only element preserved of either the fore or hind limbs and this is not entirely complete, though sufficiently well preserved to show most of the more important characters. As shown in the diagram it was found not far removed from its normal position relative to the pelvis, so that there can be no reasonable doubt that it pertains to the same skeleton. It does not differ materially from the femur in other members of the Sauropoda although as compared with the other portions of the skeleton it appears rather long and stout. There is a low and elongated fourth trochanter on the postero-internal margin midway between the proximal and distal extremities, and just external to this is a shallow concavity with a markedly rugose surface. The external condyle is larger than the internal and they are well separated by a deep intercondylar notch. The head is large and hemispherical in form but without distinct neck. The articular surface is very rugose and this rugosity is continued along the superior surface of the *greater trochanter* to the external surface of the shaft. Both the internal and external margins of the shaft of the femur curve very gently outward as shown in Fig. 14. The principal dimensions of the femur are as follows:

	mm.
Length	1275
Transverse diameter at proximal end	353
" " " distal "	309
" " " middle of shaft	207

CONCLUSIONS.

When considered together the remains upon which the present genus and species are based indicate an animal of rather unusual proportions for a member of the Sauropoda. The number of dorsals and the comparative length of the individual dorsals indicate a thoracic region proportionally longer than in *Diplodocus, Brontosaurus* or *Morosaurus*. While the cervical region appears somewhat abbreviated and the caudal region must have been remarkably short as is indicated by the reduced length of the individual verte-bræ, though this was probably made less apparent by an in-crease in the number of caudals. Judging from the femur alone the limbs were comparatively long, and the animal proportionately high and short for a Sauropod dinosaur.

HAPLOCANTHOSAURUS UTTERBACKI sp. nov.
(No. 879.)

The present species is named for Mr. W. H. Utter-back, its discoverer, and in recognition of his services to vertebrate paleontology.

Char. Sp.: It is readily distinguished from *H. priscus*, the type species of the genus by the character of the pos-terior dorsal centra which are rather more opisthocœlous than in the type species. The fully adult individual was doubtless of larger size in the present than in the first named species of the genus. But the most distinctive character is to be found in the sacrum which, in the present species, has the five neural spines normally coös-sified. The first four are coössified throughout their

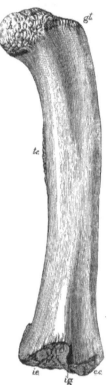

FIG. 14. Left femur of *Haplocanthosaurus priscus*, front view, seen obliquely from within (No. 572), $\frac{1}{10}$ nat. ural size. *h.*, head; *gt.*, greater trochanter; *tr.*, fourth tro-chanter; *i. e.*, internal con-dyle; *e.c.*, external condyle; *i.g.*, inter-condylar groove.

entire length, forming a long bony plate. The union between the fourth and fifth is limited to the extremities while medially they are separated by an elongated foramen. In *H. priscus* only the spines of the three anterior sacrals are coössified, those of the first and second sacrals remaining free. This difference exists notwithstanding that the type of the present species was scarcely adult, the sacral centra neither being coössified with one another nor with their neural arches. By some this character might be considered as of generic importance although I prefer to consider it as of only specific value since in all other parts of the skeleton preserved there are no distinguishing characters which could be considered as of generic value.

DESCRIPTION OF THE TYPE. (No. 879.)

The type of the present species consists of a left scapula and right coracoid, several ribs and thirty-five more or less complete vertebræ distributed as follows: Ten cervicals, thirteen dorsals, five sacrals and seven caudals. For the most part these vertebræ are complete, but in a few instances they are represented only by isolated spines and neural arches without centra, or by centra without spines and neural arches, and one anterior cervical, probably the axis or the succeeding cervical, is represented only by a portion of the neural arch. The position of these bones relative to one another as they were found in the quarry is shown within the dotted line in the upper left-hand corner of the diagram shown in Fig. 1 where the positions of the different bones are indicated as follows:

$$1 = \text{cervical } 3, \text{ placing the number of cervicals at fifteen.}$$
$$2 = \quad `` \quad 4.$$
$$3 = \quad `` \quad 8.$$
$$4 = \quad `` \quad 9.$$
$$5 = \quad `` \quad 10.$$
$$6 \text{ and } 6' = \quad `` \quad 11.$$
$$7 = \quad `` \quad 12.$$
$$8 = \quad `` \quad 13.$$
$$9 = \quad `` \quad 14.$$
$$10 = \quad `` \quad 15, \text{ or last of cervical series.}$$
$$11 \text{ and } 11' = \text{dorsal } 2.$$
$$12 = \quad `` \quad 3.$$
$$13 \text{ and } 13' = \quad `` \quad 4.$$
$$14 \text{ and } 14' = \quad `` \quad 5.$$
$$15 \text{ and } 15' = \quad `` \quad 6.$$
$$16 = \quad `` \quad 7.$$

17 = dorsal 8.

18 =   "   9.

19 =   "   10.

20 =   "   11.

21 =   "   12.

22 =   "   13.

23 =   "   14.

Sa = spines and transverse processes of sacrals; a, b, c, d, e represent respectively the spines of sacrals 1, 2, 3, 4, and 5.

24 = centrum of sacral 4.

25 =   "   "   "   5.

27 = caudal 1.

28 =   "   2.

29 =   "   3.

30 =   "   4.

31 =   "   5.

32 =   "   6.

33 =   "   7.

34 = parapophysis (sacral rib) of first sacral.

35–39 inclusive are ribs.

S = left scapula.

c = right coracoid.

Shaded bones in diagram do not pertain to *Haplocanthosaurus*.

As will appear by a critical examination of the diagram the vertebræ of the cervical and anterior dorsal regions were much scattered and displaced before finally becoming imbedded in the sands which later become solidified into the sandstones of almost granitic hardness in which they were found encased. In the following description of the vertebral column the reader should bear in mind that save for the third dorsal and the first and second caudals the centra were detached from the neural arches. Owing to the age of the individual there was as yet only a sutural union between the centra and the neural arches of the respective vertebræ. In most instances the centra, while not directly attached to their respective arches, were either found in position or only slightly removed from their normal positions relative to one another. In some instances, however, as with dorsals 2, 5 and 6, the centra and neural arches were found separated by a distance of from two to four feet, while a few vertebræ are represented by their centra or neural arches only.

The Cervicals. Plate II., Series 3 and 4.

The Third (?) Cervical (Plate II., Fig. 3, Series 4). — The most anterior vertebra of the cervical series pertaining to this skeleton I have referred to the third although it may pertain to the axis. Its fragmentary condition precludes the possibility of determining the exact position with certainty. Its position in the quarry is shown at 1 in the first diagram. It consists of the posterior portion of the neural arch with the posterior zygapophyses and it could hardly have occupied a position posterior to the third cervical although it may pertain to the axis.

The Fourth Cervical (Plate II., Fig. 4, Series 4). — A little to the right of the cervical fragment just described the present vertebra, which I interpret as the fourth cervical, was found. Its exact position in the quarry is shown at 2 on the diagram. It is essentially complete and but little distorted, though as with all the cervicals of this series the rib is disarticulated as was to be expected considering the age of the individual. The posterior zygapophyses and transverse processes are widely expanded. Near the anterior extremity and on either side of the centrum a strong process springs from the inferior lateral border. At the extremity this expands into a capitular facet for the articulation of the capitulum of the cervical rib. These processes as well as the similar, though less pronounced ones found on the succeeding cervicals may possibly be homologous with the parapophyses. In the present vertebra they are produced far below the inferior border of the centrum. The pleurocentral cavity is deep and invades the base of the ball. It is confluent with a rather deep cavity found on the superior surface of the process which supports the capitular rib facet. It is imperfectly divided into anterior and posterior cavities by a low rounded ridge which may be regarded as an incipient oblique lamina. The centrum is markedly opisthocœlous with the cavity of the posterior extremity subcircular in outline. The inferior surface of the centrum is broad and there are five shallow infracentral cavities. One of these, the posterior, is medial, and the anterior four are lateral, arranged two on either side of the central line, one at the base of and two posterior to the processes which support the rib facets. The centrum is much contracted medially.

The Eighth Cervical (Plate II., Fig. 8, Series 4). — Between the vertebra just described and the next in our series it is evident that a number are missing. I have estimated the number of missing vertebræ at three. This would make the position of this vertebra the eighth in the series, a position with which it agrees very well if we commence with the last of the series and work forward, so that I have but little doubt that this was its correct position. It is essentially complete and not badly crushed or distorted. Save for its greater size in its general form it very closely resembles the vertebra just described. The pleurocentral cavities however are more completely divided into anterior and posterior moieties by the presence of more pronounced oblique laminæ. There is a single large infracentral cavity and the cup is broader than deep. The anterior zygapophyses are supported inferiorly by short and rather slender inferior branches of the prezygapophysial laminæ while inferior branches of the diapophysial laminæ give support to the broad diapophyses which bear at their extremities the tubercular rib facets. The position of this vertebra in the quarry is shown at 3 in the diagram.

The Ninth Cervical (Plate II., Fig. 9, Series 4). — This vertebra found at 4 in the diagram of the quarry was not far removed from the preceding. It consists of the centrum with the posterior and anterior zygapophyses still in position. It is much crushed and distorted but in so far as it is possible to determine, it agrees fairly well with what we should expect to find in the ninth cervical. It has been erroneously drawn as complete in Plate II., Fig. 9.

The Tenth, Eleventh, Twelfth and Thirteenth Cervicals (Plate II., Figs. 10, 11, 12, 13, Series 3). — These four vertebræ are in each instance well-nigh perfect and they display such a gradation of progressive characters that there can be no doubt as to their constituting a continuous series.

The neural spines and posterior zygapophyses become successively more elevated as we proceed backward in the series. The spines however show no tendency to divide, there being scarcely an emargination at the summit even in the last of the four. The posterior zygapophyses become successively more expanded and the suprapostzygapophysial cavities become deeper and broader. The position of these vertebræ in the quarry was as follows: The tenth was found at 5, the neural arch and spine of the eleventh was found at 6, and the centrum at 6', the twelfth is shown at 7 and the thirteenth at 8.

The Fourteenth Cervical (Plate II., Fig. 14, Series 3). — Only the centrum of this vertebra was recovered; it was found at 9 on the diagram. It is considerably crushed, especially anteriorly but there is no doubt that it was a cervical and that its position was posterior to the thirteenth. Its size, length and general characters indicate that it belonged immediately behind the thirteenth I have, therefore, regarded it as the fourteenth.

The Fifteenth Cervical (Plate II., Fig. 15, Series 3). — This is represented by a well-preserved neural arch and spine without centrum found at 10 as shown on the diagram. The difference between this spine and that of the thirteenth is such as to preclude the possibility of its pertaining to the fourteenth or immediately succeeding cervical. I have, therefore, assigned it to the fifteenth or last cervical, with which it agrees very well when compared with the spine of that vertebra in *H. priscus* where there can be no question as to the proper position relative to the dorsals. Moreover if the spine of the fourteenth cervical in *H. priscus* be interposed between the present spine and that of the thirteenth cervical in the present skeleton they are seen to form a well-graduated series leaving little doubt that the positions are assigned to the various vertebræ of this region of the cervical series in the skeleton under consideration are correct. The neural spine is faintly emarginate at the apex. The depth of the emargination is 4 mm.

The Dorsals. (Plate II., Series 1 and 2.)

The Second Dorsal (Plate II., Fig. 2, series 2.) There is in the vertebral series of the present skeleton no vertebra corresponding to the first dorsal in *H. priscus*. That vertebra is apparently unrepresented in the present series. The neural arch and spine found at 11′ fits fairly well on the centrum found at 11 and I have considered them as pertaining to the second dorsal. As to the neural spine and arch there can be little doubt as to this determination, but as to the position of the centrum, it is by no means certain that it does not pertain to the first rather than the second dorsal. Indeed as regards the length and form of the centrum, character of the pleurocentral cavities, and position of the capitular rib facet, it would appear to more properly pertain to the first dorsal than to the second, while the widely separated position (about four feet) in which they (the centra and neural arch) were found might be taken as an indication that they pertain to different vertebræ. I have associated this centrum and spine in the same vertebra for no other reason than that when adjusted to one another they seem to agree fairly well. I believe it quite possible, even probable, that the centrum pertains to the first dorsal. As regards the neural arch and spine however, after comparing them with those of the first dorsal in *H. priscus*, there can be no reasonable doubt but that they pertain to the second dorsal. This position is indicated by the character of the anterior branch of the horizontal lamina which is much less modified to give support to the scapula than in the first dorsal of *H. priscus*. The articular surfaces of the postzygapophyses have assumed a more perpendicular position in anticipation of the hyposphene-hypantrum method of articulation that obtains in the median and posterior dorsals. The neural spine is passing from the widely expanded scoop-like element seen in the posterior cervicals and dorsal one to the simpler form characteristic of the median and posterior dorsals. The superior branches of the postzygapophysial lamina continue, however, confluent with the neural spine, extending to its very apex and enclosing laterally a rather deep cavity which, nevertheless, is much less deep than in the last cervical of this series or the first dorsal of *H. priscus*. As in the succeeding dorsals the distance between the anterior and posterior zygapophyses is much abbreviated. There is a very faint emargination at the apex of the neural spine with a depth of only 7 mm.

The Third Dorsal (Plate II., Fig. 3, Series 2).—This vertebra lay on end as shown at 12 in the first diagram. Owing to the position in which it lay in the quarry its centrum was much shortened by the pressure to which it was subjected, the ball having been forced down into the pleuro-central cavities and the whole centrum telescoped as it were. Fortunately the neural arch and spine are in a splendid state of preservation. They are still held in position with the centrum, though the sutures are very distinct. The spine when compared with that of the preceding vertebra is much modified in the direction of the conditions that obtain in the succeeding dorsals. It has assumed a nearly vertical position instead of being inclined forward as in the preceding dorsals and cervicals.

It is very much compressed antero-posteriorly and is still connected with the posterior zygapophyses by the superior branches of the post-zygapophysial laminæ. In the present vertebra however this lamina does not run obliquely upward and backward in a direct and straight line from the zygapophysis to the top of the neural spine as in the preceding dorsals and the cervicals, but it extends backward, rising but little until it reaches the vertical plane of the anterior surface of the spine when it rises vertically as a thin narrow lamina ascending to the apex of the spine. The degree of differentiation in the neural spines of this and the immediately preceding vertebra is the most marked of any of the vertebræ even in this region where the characters of the different vertebræ are seen to change so rapidly. The apex of this spine is also faintly emarginate, the notch having a depth of 9 mm. The position of the capitular rib facet is at the supero-anterior angle of the pleurocentral cavity.

The Fourth Dorsal (Plate II., Fig. 4, Series 2). —The centrum and spine of this vertebra lay as shown at 13 and 13′ in the diagram. They are both well preserved, and the nature of the spine and transverse processes demonstrate beyond a reasonable doubt that its position in the vertebral column was immediately posterior to the vertebra just described. The spine is now quite perpendicular and more elevated. It is much compressed antero-posteriorly but somewhat expanded transversely. Its anterior surface is transversely convex, the posterior is concave, forming a long, shallow trough or scoop not nearly so deep as in the preceding vertebræ. The transverse processes in this and the immediately preceding vertebra are assuming a more elevated position, the neural arches are becoming higher and the transverse processes instead of being horizontal are directed successively more and more obliquely upward as in the succeeding dorsals.

The Fifth, Sixth, Seventh, Eighth, Ninth, Tenth and Eleventh Dorsals (Plate II., Figs. 5–11, Series 1 and 2). — The neural arches and spines of all these vertebræ were found interlocked by their zygapophyses as shown in the diagram from 14–20 inclusive. The centra of the fifth and sixth had become detached and lay as shown at 14′ and 15′. The remaining centra were in position at the base of their respective spines. The neural spines, transverse processes, capitular rib facets, neural arches, etc., form a regularly graudated series except that the capitular rib facet of the sixth is much larger than in the other vertebræ. The neural arch, spine and transverse processes of the fifth were much injured, but the spine is nearly entire and it is evident that it pertained to the vertebra immediately posterior to that just described as indicated also by the centrum. The spine is still compressed anteroposteriorly but decidedly deeper in that direction than the spine of the vertebra just described. In the spine of the succeeding or sixth dorsal the transverse and anteroposterior diameters are subequal. A hyposphene-hypantrum articulation begins with the sixth dorsal and continues throughout the remaining dorsal series.

The Twelfth, Thirteenth, and Fourteenth Dorsals (Plate II., Figs. 12–14, Series 1). — These vertebræ do not differ materially from the same vertebræ already described as pertaining to the type of *H. priscus.* They were found as shown at 21, 22 and 23 in the diagram, interposed between the series just described and the anterior extremity of the sacrum. As shown in the diagram the neural arches were in position relative to one another but the centra were a little removed from their normal positions. They are all in a nearly perfect condition.

If the reader has followed carefully the above description of the dorsals pertaining to the present skeleton together with those which pertained to the type of *H. priscus* and will examine the accompanying figures it will have become apparent that the complete dorsal series in *Haplocanthosaurus* must have consisted of not less than fourteen free vertebræ while it is scarcely possible that there were more than fourteen. This is a very marked increase over the number (ten) which is believed to have formed the complement of free dorsals in *Diplodocus, Brontosaurus* and *Morosaurus.* Nor does this increase in the number of dorsals in the present genus seem to have been made at the expense of the cervical series, for as near as we can judge, *Haplocanthosaurus,* like *Diplodocus,* was provided with fifteen cervicals. Our determination of the number of cervicals however does not rest on anything like so good a basis as does our determination of the number of dorsals but there can be little doubt but that the number of presacrals in the present genus exceeded that of the same series in *Diplodocus*.

The Sacrals. (Figs. 15, 16 and 20.)

The sacrum of the present skeleton differs considerably from that of the type of *H. priscus*. Its position in the quarry is shown in the diagram at *Sa*. Only the neural spines and diapophyses, the parapophyses of the right side and the centra of the fourth and fifth sacrals are preserved. The neural spines of the first, second, third and fourth sacrals are confluent and firmly coössified throughout their entire length, while the spine of the fifth is coössified only at the top and the bottom with that of the fourth sacral, and medially there is an elongated foramen between these spines shown at *f* in fig. 15. The spines of the two anterior sacrals rise nearly perpendicular, those of the third and fourth are directed somewhat backward, while that of the fifth is again directed forward to meet at the apex that of the fourth sacral. The spines of the first, second, third and fourth sacrals bear diapophysial laminæ, and at the summit these expand into prominent rugosities.

The diapophyses of the first and second sacrals are directed outward, forward and a little upward, nearly parallel to one another. Those of the succeeding sacrals are directed outward, backward and a little upward, parallel to one another, but that of the third meets that of the second in an acute angle at the base of the diapophysial lamina, forming a letter V with the apex directed toward the spine. The diapophysis of the third sacral is formed by the union of branches from the diapophysial laminæ of the second and third sacral spines.

All the parapophyses (sacral ribs) of the right side are present and nearly complete. They all show sutural surfaces for articulation with the sacral centra and with the ilium. The parapophyses are shown in position in the view of the sacrum from the right side seen in Fig. 15, while comparative front views of the individual parapophyses are given in Fig. 16, *a, b, c, d, e,* which represents the series from the first to the fifth, respectively. Of the five parapophyses the first is the more slender. It is triangular in outline, with an emarginate base describing a nearly complete semicircle. It may be described as composed of a horizontal and ascending branch. The surface for contact with the centrum is not greatly expanded. There are two surfaces for contact with the ilium, one inferior, the other superior and separated by a distance of about 215 mm. The inferior of these surfaces is more pronounced and both show prominent rugosities. The anterior surface of this bone is convex, the posterior concave. Between the inferior and superior surfaces for contact with the ilium there was an elongated foramen enclosed externally by the ilium and internally by the ascending branch.

In the parapophysis of the second sacral the horizontal branch has become very strong and much expanded at either extremity for contact with the centrum and ilium. The ascending branch is broad but very thin, and presents at its extremity only a small rugosity for contact with the ilium. The foramen between it and the ilium was broader than that separating the same branch of the preceding parapophysis. Immediately above the surface for contact with the centrum there is a rugosity which doubtless gave support to the descending branch of the diapophysis,

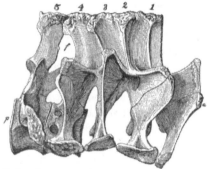

FIG. 15. Sacrum of *Haplocanthosaurus utterbacki*, seen from right side, ⅒ natural size. *a*, anterior extremity; *p*, posterior extremity; *1, 2, 3, 4, 5*, spines of first to fifth sacrals; *f*, foramen between spines of fourth and fifth sacrals.

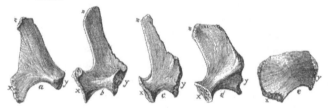

FIG. 16. Anterior view of disarticulated parapophyses (sacral ribs) of *Haplocanthosaurus utterbacki*, ⅒ natural size. *a* to *e*, first to fifth respectively; *y*, surface for contact with sacral centrum; *x*, inferior surface for contact with ilium; *z*, superior surface for contact with ilium.

but it would appear that the diapophysis and parapophysis were not in contact throughout their entire length, but were separated for a considerable distance by an elongated foramen. The external extremity of the horizontal branch is greatly expanded transversely so as to unite with the same element in the succeeding parapophysis, to form the acetabular bar and give additional support to the ilium.

The parapophysis of the third sacral differs from that just described in its shorter horizontal branch and narrower and more slender ascending branch. The shortening of the horizontal branch is of course brought about by the inward curvature of the ilium in the region of the acetabulum.

The fourth parapophysis differs from all the preceding in its widely expanded ascending branch which curves very gently backward. The horizontal branch is stout and longer than that of the third parapophysis.

The fifth and last parapophysis differs from all the preceding in the absence of any ascending branch. The horizontal branch is greatly expanded vertically, and the articular surface for the ilium is elongate so as to give support to the ischiac peduncle and posterior blade of the ilium. The principal characters of the parapophyses are well shown in the accompanying figures.

Only the centra of the fourth and fifth sacrals are preserved. Fortunately these are well preserved. The parapophyses of the right side fit very well when adjusted to their respective vertebræ. Neither of these vertebræ show any marked enlargement of the neural canal. They are both constricted medially, and the distal extremity of the fifth is considerably expanded for contact with the first caudal. The centrum of the fifth sacral is decidedly heavier than that of the fourth.

The principal measurements of the different sacral elements in the type of the present species are as follows:

	mm.
Distance along crest of the five coössified sacral spines	460
" " " " four anterior " "	375
" from anterior zygapophyses of first sacral to posterior zygapophyses of fifth sacral	575
Expanse of diapophysis of third sacral	375
Greatest length of horizontal branch of first parapophysis	213
" height of ascending " " " "	300
" length of horizontal " " second " "	146
" height of ascending " " " "	300
" length of horizontal " " third " "	128
" height of ascending " " " "	277
" length of horizontal " " fourth " "	150
" height of ascending " " " "	250
" length of horizontal " " fifth " "	225
Length of fourth sacral centrum	132
Depth " " " " at posterior end	166
Width " " " " " " "	132
Length " fifth " " " " " "	120
Depth " " " " " " "	182
Width " " " " " " "	181

The Caudals. (Plate II., Series 5.)

Only the seven anterior caudals are preserved in the type of the present species and these differ very little from the same vertebræ in *H. priscus*, except that the transverse processes are less well developed and not so much expanded supero-inferiorly. Owing to the age of the individual the neural arches and transverse processes are not coössified with their respective centra although those of the first two are still held in place. The neural spines are short and stout and very rugose. That of the first is curved rather strongly backward. All the centra are very short and biconcave. The anterior zygapophyses are acutely wedge-shaped and extend well forward with the articular surfaces facing decidedly more inward than upward. The posterior zygapophyses are only flattened surfaces at the bases of the neural spines. The transverse processes are suturally connected both with the centra and the neural arches.

The Vertebral Formula.

From the foregoing descriptions of those portions of the vertebral column preserved in the type of the present species and in that of *H. priscus* it will have become apparent that we must await future discoveries to determine with accuracy the vertebral formula of *Haplocanthosaurus*. The number of sacrals however may be considered as being definitely fixed at five, while the number of dorsals could not have been less than fourteen, thirteen of which are represented in the skeleton constituting the type of *H. utterbacki*. In this skeleton it would appear that only the first dorsal is missing, and fortunately that vertebra in the type of *H. priscus* was found interlocked by its zygapophyses with the last cervical. Although the various vertebræ in the anterior dorsal region of the type of *H. utterbacki* were for the most part found in such a scattered and disarticulated condition as to afford little direct evidence concerning the exact positions relative to one another which they occupied in the skeleton during the life of the animal, yet a close examination and careful study of the vertebræ has convinced me that there are no duplicates among the thirteen dorsals described and that there can be no question but that all of the thirteen are dorsals and that they pertained to the skeleton of one and the same individual. That the first dorsal is wanting in this skeleton is shown by a careful comparison of the neural arch and spine of the most anterior of this series with that of the known first dorsal in *H. priscus*, from which, as has been shown in the descriptions, it differs materially and in the direction of those characters which we should expect in the succeeding or second dorsal. For these reasons I have referred this spine to the second dorsal although the centrum which was found detached and separated, but which in the description and figure I have associated with this spine may, as I have already remarked, pertain to the first dorsal. I do not think it at all probable that more than one dorsal is missing from the series in *H. utterbacki* and it is with a feeling of considerable confidence that I place the number of dorsals in this species at least, at fourteen. Fully realizing the character of the evidences upon which I have arrived at this conclusion I have spared no pains to present to the student all the evidence furnished by the material at my command, both as regards its anatomical characters and the position in which the different bones were found in the quarry. Aided by the accompanying diagrams and with the type material at his disposal the future student will be in full possession of all the evidence in the case and will therefore be in a position to decide for himself as to the worth of my conclusions.

In placing the number of free dorsals at fourteen I am fully aware that this is a considerable advance over the number that has of late come very generally to be considered as characteristic of other members of the Sauropoda (*Diplodocus, Brontosaurus, Morosaurus*). Considering however the less specialized nature of the present genus and the great differences seen, in other important characters, when compared with the genera just mentioned I do not consider this increase in the number of dorsals as at all remarkable, for it is not at all impossible that the earlier ancestors of *Diplodocus, Brontosaurus and Morosaurus* were provided with an equal number of free dorsals and that the reduction to ten in each of those genera may be regarded as a specialized character attendant upon and which took place along with that remarkable specialization which, as is well known, they must have undergone in other respects and which is most marked in that exceedingly complicated arrangement of laminæ and buttresses seen in the dorsal and cervical vertebræ of those genera.

It will doubtless have been remarked that in describing the cervicals I have placed the number of vertebræ of this region at fifteen, the number present in *Diplodocus*. It must be admitted, however, that the material at hand does not afford a very reliable basis for determining the number of cervicals and I should not be at all surprised if the actual number of cervicals in *Haplocanthosaurus* should prove to be one or two less than in *Diplodocus*. In placing the number at fifteen, as in the latter genus, I assume that *Haplocanthosaurus* was provided with four more presacrals than was *Diplodocus*. While my estimate of the number of cervicals in the present genus may prove to be too great, it is hardly possible that it will be reduced by more than two. This would still give to *Haplocanthosaurus* two more presacrals than are present in *Diplodocus*. It would thus appear that in the various genera of the Sauropoda the number of presacrals differed and that the number of cervicals is not entirely dependent upon an increase or decrease in the number of dorsals in any genus within the group. Still it is easily conceivable that in any genus or species the presacral formula might vary, without increasing the total number of presacrals in the individual, according as the exact position in the presacral series at which the change from cervicals to dorsals took place, and I am inclined to the opinion that as a rule in any given genus of the Sauropoda where marked specialization has taken place, there has been a tendency to increase the number of cervicals at the expense of the dorsal series, due to the gradual shifting of the pectoral girdle from a more advanced to a more posterior position, by which process anterior dorsals have been transformed into posterior cervicals and the cervical region considerably elongated at the expense of the dorsal. An extreme instance of this is to be seen in *Diplodocus carnegii* where the disparity in length in the neck and dorsum, probably due primarily to the increased number of cervicals and decreased number of dorsals, has been still further emphasized by the proportionate length of the individual vertebræ in the two series.

If, as does not seem improbable, the total number of presacrals was ever decreased in any genus it would appear to have been more readily accomplished by the successive elimination of the less specialized, or at least more simple, anterior cervicals than by the disappearance of the extremely complicated dorsals. Nor does it seem probable or even possible that such a decrease in the number of presacrals could have been brought about by the gradual shifting of the pelvic girdle to a more anterior position. Such an hypothesis presupposes the addition to the sacrum of successive posterior dorsals and the liberating of posterior sacrals as anterior caudals, an hypothesis which to the present writer appears unworthy of serious consideration. As to the total number of caudals in the present genus we have nothing upon which to base anything like a reliable estimate. From the character of the posterior five or six of the series of nineteen anterior caudals in the type of *H. priscus* we may judge that while the tail was relatively short the number of caudals was considerable and probably not less than forty. The increased number of caudals is indicated in the first place by the character of the chevron found attached to the thirteenth caudal and which, as already remarked, resembles in general form the chevron of a caudal occupying a more anterior position in *Diplodocus*. Moreover, the very gradual change which is seen to be taking place in the posterior caudals of the series preserved in the type of *H. priscus* indicates a very considerable number of posterior caudals as having intervened between the last of the series and the end of the tail. The extreme shortness of the centra in the caudals of *Haplocanthosaurus* may be considered as sufficient proof that the tail was proportionately rather short as compared with that of *Diplodocus*.

After a careful consideration of all the evidence at hand the following is submitted as the approximate vertebral formula in the present genus. *Cervicals 15; Dorsals 14; Sacrals 5; Caudals not less than 40.*

Below I give the principal dimensions of the several vertebræ pertaining to the type of the present species. Some of these dimensions have been materially altered by crushing in such manner as to cause apparent inconsistencies. They should only be taken as representing in a general way the dimensions of the various vertebræ.

In column 1 the greatest expanse of the transverse processes is given, column 2, greatest length of centrum; column 3, transverse diameter of centrum at posterior extremity; column 4, hight of neural spines above middle of inferior border of centra in presacrals and above inferior border of posterior end in postsacrals.

	mm. 1.	in.	mm. 2.	in.	mm. 3.	in	mm. 4.	in.
4. Cervical.	154	6 1/16	143	5 5/8	61	2 3/8	136	5 3/8
8. "	210	8 1/4	220	8 5/8	103	4	192	7 1/2
9. "	?	?	?	?	?	?	?	?
10. "	192	7 1/2	243	9 1/2	102	4	196	7 3/4
11. "	204	8	238	9 3/8	111	4 3/8	225	8 1/4
12. "	234	9 1/4	264	10 3/8	113	4 3/8	255	10
13. "	258	10 1/8	292	11 1/2	125	4 7/8	265	10 7/16
14. "			268	10 1/2	112	4 3/8		
15. "	320	12 1/4						
2. Dorsal.	390	15 1/4	200	8	125	4 7/8	368	14 1/2
3. "	374	14 3/4	120	4 3/4	127	5	422	16 5/8
4. "	395	15 5/8	150	5 7/8	115	4 1/2	435	17 1/8
5. "	390	15 3/8	135	5 1/4	124	4 7/8	483	19
6. "			150	5 7/8	109	4 1/4	492	19 3/8
7. "			135	5 1/4	116	4 7/16	500	19 3/4
8. "			170	6 5/8	102	4	550	21 5/8
9. "			152	6	137	5 3/8	540	21 1/4
10. "			148	5 3/4	145	5 11/16	558	22
11. "			143	5 5/8	175	6 7/8	535	21
12. "			137	5 3/8	169	6 5/8	549	21 5/8
13. "			135	5 5/16	178	7	560	22
14. "			125	4 11/16	170	6 3/4	552	21 3/4
1. Caudal.	350	13 3/4	115	4 1/2	160	6 3/8	425	16 3/4
2. "	310	12 1/4	80	3 1/4	166	6 1/2	410	16 1/8
3. "			75	3	165	6 1/2	393	15 1/2
4. "			83	3 1/4	157	6 1/4	355	14 3/8
5. "			83	3 1/4	143	5 5/8	346	13 5/8
6. "			90	3 1/2	130	5 1/8	331	13
7. "			85	3 3/8	133	5 1/4	313	12 1/4

The Pectoral Arch. (Figs. 17, 18, 19.)

Only the left scapula (Figs. 17 and 18) and right coracoid (Fig. 19) are preserved.

The Coracoid (Fig. 19). — The external surface of this bone is regularly but gently convex. The internal surface is concave. The anterior and inferior margins are for the most part thin, but at the antero-inferior angle the margin is thickened and presents an elongated rugosity shown at *a* 140 mm. in length and 40 mm. in greatest breadth, probably for the ligamentous articulation of the sternum. The surface for articulation with the scapula has a length of 150 mm. and a greatest breadth, at its junction with the glenoid border, of 90 mm. The coracoid forms about one half the glenoid cavity and the glenoidal surface meets the surface for articulation with the scapula at an obtuse angle. Between the inferior margin of the glenoid cavity and the inferior border there is a rather deep notch in the pos-

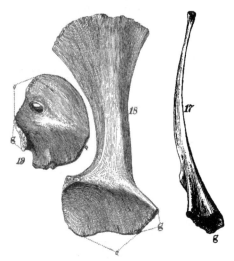

FIG. 17.   Posterior view of left scapula of *H. utterbacki* ; *g*, glenoid surface, $\frac{1}{10}$ natural size.

FIG. 18.   External view of same ; *g*, glenoid surface ; *c*, surface for coracoid.

FIG. 19.   External view of right coracoid of *H. utterbacki* ; *s*, surface for scapula ; *g*, glenoid surface ; *a*, rugosity for supposed contact with sternal, $\frac{1}{10}$ natural size.

terior border of the coracoid. The foramen is large and is situated about 35 mm. beneath the coraco-scapular suture. It is elliptical in outline with the vertical diameter the longer. The dimensions are 57 mm. for the vertical and 30 mm. for the transverse diameter at the external opening. The distance from the glenoid border to the sutural surface at the antero-inferior angle is 295 mm. The distance from the postero-inferior angle to the anterior border just beneath the coraco-scapular suture is 350 mm.

The Scapula (Figs. 17 and 18). — The scapula displays the extreme development of that form shown in *Morosaurus* with broadly expanded extremities. I cannot describe the characters better than to give the measurements. The breadth of the scapula at the proximal end is 372 mm., at the distal [6] 396 mm. and in the middle only 137 mm. Between the spine and the coraco-scapular suture there is a broad but shallow cavity on the external surface of the scapula. Above this ridge, however, the external surface of the scapula is convex in all directions. The total length of the scapula from its superior or proximal end to the coraco-scapular suture is 800 mm. The accompanying figures show very well the form and principal characters of this element.

From the foregoing description of the types of the two species of *Haplocanthosaurus* at present known and from the accompanying measurements and figures it will appear that as compared with *Diplodocus* the present genus was represented by animals with the thorax somewhat more elongated and with neck and tail relatively shorter than those which obtained in representatives of the former genus. While, judging from the femur, the only element of the limbs at present available, the appendicular skeleton was relatively strong when compared with the axial.

Distinctive Generic Characters.

The principal characters distinguishing the genus *Haplocanthosaurus* may be summarized as follows:

FIRST. — *Neural spines short and simple (not branched) throughout the entire vertebral column.*

SECOND. — *Neural spines of the anterior sacrals coössified, forming an elongated bony plate.*

THIRD. — *Height of neural arches in posterior dorsals exceeding length of neural spines.*

FOURTH. — *Transverse processes of the anterior and mid-dorsal regions inclined upward and outward instead of directly outward.*

The two species described above may be distinguished as follows by their respective sacra.

HAPLOCANTHOSAURUS PRISCUS. — *With neural spines of the three anterior sacrals coössified, those of the two posterior remaining free.*

HAPLOCANTHOSAURUS UTTERBACKI. — *With neural spines of the four anterior sacrals coössified throughout their entire length and with that of the fifth sacral at the top and bottom.*

Taxonomy.

All systematists will, I think, agree with me in placing the present genus among the *Sauropoda*. The scapula, coracoid, pelvis and sacrum, as well as the presence of large pleurocentral cavities in the presacral centra, together furnish

[6] I consider that end of the scapula which opposes the humerus as the distal.

conclusive evidence as to its affinities with that group of the *Dinosauria*. Nevertheless there are a few characters, such as the elongated neural arches and comparatively short and absolutely simple neural spines of the dorsal and posterior cervical series, the conformation of the transverse processes and position of the capitular rib facets, which are different from any other known member of the *Sauropoda* of North America and are more nearly paralleled by the characters which exist in the vertebræ of this region in some members of the *Predentata*, more especially in *Stegosaurus*, where, as in *Haplocanthosaurus*, the neural spines are short as compared with the elevated neural arches from the summit of which, in each case in the posterior dorsals, the transverse processes spring and diverge from the bases of the perpendicular spines at angles of about 45° instead of being directed horizontally as is the usual manner in the *Sauropoda*. The presence of characters so similar as those just mentioned in representatives of the *Sauropoda* and the *Predentata* while certainly not indicative of any very close relationship may perhaps be considered as evidence of a remote common ancestry for the two groups. If this view be taken, these characters possessed in common would be considered not as parallel or analogous characters developed independently in each instance, but as persistent primitive characters which were present in their remote but common ancestors. As the development of the two groups progressed and they became more and more differentiated, such characters proved advantageous and became more emphasized in the *Predentata* while in the *Sauropoda*, where for some reason they were not particularly advantageous, they were gradually eliminated and disappeared altogether in the more highly specialized forms though persisting in the more primitive *Haplocanthosaurus*. It is by the presence in common, among the *Sauropoda*, *Theropoda* and *Predentata*, of such characters as those just described, that the student of the Dinosauria will find the most trustworthy evidence as to the actual relationships or want of relationships in the three groups. Not until a considerable number of genera within each group are known from a detailed study of the osteology of fairly complete skeletons will it be possible to pronounce with any degree of certainty even upon the question as to whether the Dinosauria is a natural group as maintained by Marsh or an entirely unnatural one, without any right to existence, into which has been thrown three distinct groups, totally dissimilar and with nothing in common, as was held by the late Dr. George Baur. In the discussion of this question however there are several points which should be constantly kept in mind by the advocates of either view. Among these are :

FIRST.— Those who are opposed to considering the *Dinosauria* as a natural group should bear in mind the great antiquity that must be accorded to that group when considered as constituting a single group. Evidence of such antiquity is found not alone in the great diversity exhibited by the three subdivisions into which the group as a whole has been divided but by the diversity and specialization exhibited by the different families, genera and species within each of these three subdivisions, As yet we know comparatively little of the earlier *Dinosauria* and the group if in reality it be a natural one is at present represented in our museums for the most part only by the later and more specialized forms. Of the *Sauropoda* we know only those forms which lived just prior to their extermination when they were already highly specialized. Consider for a moment the enormous time interval which must have been necessary for the development of a reptile like *Diplodocus.* Yet his remains are found associated in the same quarry with those of *Haplocanthosaurus.* the most primitive Sauropod known, and the entire range of the Sauropoda throughout the geological column in North America so far as at present known is limited to certain horizons in the Jurassic or Lower Cretaceous of some authors, with a vertical thickness never exceeding a few hundred feet, and from the top to the bottom of which there are always found forms which are highly specialized, conclusive proof that the paleontological record is exceedingly incomplete as regards this group.

Although the time distribution of the *Theropoda* and *Predentata* as we now know it is more considerable than that of the *Sauropoda* yet it is by no means complete and we know little of the earlier forms of either of these divisions. The wonder therefore is not that the three divisions as we now know them should show so little in common, but rather that, considering their great antiquity and early differentiation, they should have continued to possess in common even such characters as they do show.

SECOND.—Although due weight should be given to every marked and important difference in structure it should nevertheless be borne in mind that every character possessed in common by these three divisions or by any two of them should be considered as an evidence of relationship until definitely proved to be fortuituous or as having been developed independently in each instance.

THIRD.—It is in the, as yet undiscovered, earlier and more generalized members of these groups that we must look for those characters which will throw most light on this question. If future explorations should be rewarded by the discovery in the early or middle Trias of a considerable number of representatives of each of the groups which we now refer to the *Dinosauria*, and if together they were shown to possess many characters in common and to approach one another much more nearly than do the Jurassic and Cretaceous forms, this evidence would be considered as strongly favoring the including of them all in a single group, the *Dinosauria*. If on the other hand they were found to show little in common or were even more widely separated than are the later forms from the Jurassic and Cretaceous then there could be no reasonable grounds for considering the Dinosauria as a natural group and it would become necessary to discard that term, at least in the sense in which it is at present used.

Since however as has been shown in *Haplocanthosaurus*, the *Sauropoda* and *Predentata* do possess certain important anatomical characters in common and since in this the most generalized genus of the group at present known the relationships between these two groups are more apparent than in the more specialized genera, *Diplodocus*, *Brontosaurus*, etc. It is reasonable to suppose that in the yet undiscovered but still more generalized forms greater similarity in structure will be found. Moreover from our present knowledge the relationships between the *Sauropoda*, *Predentata* and *Theropoda*, as has already been pointed out by Marsh, is indicated by a number of important characters possessed in common such as :

"1. *Teeth with distinct roots either fixed in more or less distinct sockets or in longitudinal grooves, never ankylosed, no palatal teeth.*

"2. *Skull with superior and inferior temporal arches.*

"3. *Double-headed cervical and thoracic ribs.*

"4. *Sacral vertebræ coössified and more numerous than in other reptiles, seldom less than five.*

"5. *Ilium extended in front of acetabulum, in the construction of which latter the ilium, ischium and pubis take part.*

"6. *Fibula complete.*

"7. *The reduction in the number of digits commences with the fifth.*"

The present author is, therefore, of the opinion that the Dinosauria should be regarded as a valid and distinct group for the exact definition and description of which we must await further discoveries as also for definite proof that the different groups now included in it are actually related.

Admitting that the Dinosauria do constitute a natural group we have next to consider the rank that should be accorded to it in any general scheme looking to a classification of the Animal Kingdom as a whole. Here again we find there has been great diversity of opinion. Without reviewing the various opinions that have at various times been expressed upon this subject it would appear to the present author, that, in consideration of the diversity in form, structure and habit which are found withing this group where some members are carnivorous and others herbivorous, some quadrupedal and others bipedal, some heavily armored and others unarmored and with all the many and diverse anatomical characters shown in their osteology which might reasonably be expected from such diversity of habits, there would seem good reasons for considering the Dinosauria as deserving of the rank of a subclass of the Reptilia comparable for example with the Metatheria of the Mammalia and divisible into three orders for each of which several names have been proposed by various authors. Of all these, those proposed by Marsh appear to the present writer to be the most appropriate, these are:

1. THE THEROPODA; *Embracing all the carnivorous dinosarus.*

2. THE SAUROPODA; *Embracing all the herbivorous forms in which the predentary is wanting.*

3. THE PREDENTATA; *Embracing all the herbivorous forms in which the predentary is present.*

In accepting the terms *Theropoda* and *Sauropoda* rather than *Megalosauria* and *Cetiosauria* I do so out of regard for the more comprehensive nature of those terms as used by Marsh. The latter terms as used originally by Fitzinger (*Megalosauri*), 1843, and Seeley, 1874, respectively, I consider of subordinal rank only. *Predentata*, Marsh, is preferable to *Orthopoda*, Cope, because it is in no sense coördinate with the latter but a much more comprehensive term. Cope's *Orthopoda* and the *Ornithopoda* of Marsh (not Huxley) are more nearly synonymous.

Some authorities have considered the *Sauropoda* of Marsh (1878) as a synonym of the *Opisthocœlia* of Owen (1859). But this appears to me quite unwarranted. For the latter term, although having priority, was never adequately defined by Owen. It was originally proposed as a suborder of the *Crocodilia*[7] and was characterized as embracing members of that group with opisthocœlous dorsal and cervical vertebræ. Owens' original definition of the *Opisthocœlia* was as follows: "The small group of *Crocidilia*, so called, is an artificial one based upon more or less of the anterior trunk vertebræ being united by ball-and-socket joints, but having the ball in front, instead of, as in modern crocodiles, behind." As is now well known, the above character in no way distinguishes these dinosaurs from members of either the *Theropoda* or *Predentata*, and on the same page, in defining the order *Dinosauria*, Owen describes the cervical vertebræ as being opisthocœlous in some species. It is thus clear that Owen not only did not adequately define his proposed suborder *Opisthocœlia*, but that he did not recognize its real relationships as being with the *Dinosauria* rather than the *Crocodilia*. The character given distinguishes it from the *Procœlia* or true *Crocodilia*, but should be considered as uniting it with, rather than separating it from, the Theropod and Predentate dinosaurs, for as has already

[7] See Report 29th meeting Brit. Assoc. Adv. Sci., 1859, pp. 164, 165.

been stated this character is possessed in common by members of both these groups. While *Cetiosaurus* is an undoubted member of the *Sauropoda* (Opisthocœlia) as determined by Owen, this fact does not serve to define properly the latter term which remains a *nomen nudum*, while the *Sauropoda*, proposed and defined by Marsh in the *American Journal of Science* for November, 1878, page 412, should be accepted as the first adequately defined name for this group of dinosaurs.

In proposing the term Sauropoda for this group of dinosaurs in the paper just cited Marsh adds :

"The most marked characters of this group are as follows:

"1. The fore and hind limbs are nearly equal in size.

"2. The carpal and tarsal bones are distinct.

"3. The feet are plantigrade, with five toes on each foot.

"4. The precaudal vertebræ contain large cavities, apparently pneumatic.

"5. The neural arches are united to the centra by suture.

"6. The sacral vertebræ do not exceed four, and each supports its own transverse process.

"7. The chevrons have free articular extremities.

"8. The pubes unite in front by ventral symphysis.

"9. The third trochanter is rudimentary or wanting.

"10. The limb bones are without medullary cavities."

Although the subsequent discovery of more complete material has shown that No. 6 of these characters is erroneous, and that certain others are possessed in common by some members of the Theropoda and Predentata, yet Marsh's original definition still remains fairly diagnostic of the group, and the term *Sauropoda* should, therefore, it appears to the present writer, be accepted.

Whether this group should be considered as of only subordinal rank, as originally proposed by Marsh or as of ordinal value as considered in his later publications, is a question concerning which there is at present no unanimity of opinion. Each student must, for the present at least, determine for himself the rank to be assigned such groups, and such decisions will necessarily be determined by, and vary according as certain characters are considered as of greater or less importance by the different investigators. Without going into an extended discussion of this question the present author feels warranted in considering the *Sauropoda* as a distinct order, comparable for instance with the Ungulata among the Eutherian Mammalia, or the Diprodontia among the Metatheria, according to Gadow's "Classification of the Vertebrata."

It now remains to discuss the relations of the genus *Haplocanthosaurus* to the various genera and families of the Sauropoda that have already been proposed.

This will be the more easily understood if we first notice briefly the principal characters of the different families within that order.

Marsh has divided the Sauropoda into six families which he has named as follows: (1) *Atlantosauridæ*; (2) *Diplodocidæ*; (3) *Morosauridæ*; (4) *Pleurocœlidæ*; (5) *Titanosauridæ*; (6) *Cardiodontidæ*.

As already stated in my memoir on *Diplodocus*, when discussing the taxonomy of that genus, it is not improbable that the number of families recognized by Marsh is too great and should be somewhat reduced. However it would seem premature to attempt a revision of the genera and families of this group until the large and splendid collections recently brought together by the Carnegie Museum, the American Museum and the Field Columbian Museum have been thoroughly studied. It is safe to say, however, that no such reduction in the number of families as that proposed in the second volume of the English edition of Zittel's " Text-Book of Paleontology " will become necessary. Nor will it be found necessary or desirable to associate in the same family genera so different as are *Brontosaurus* and *Morosaurus* as was done in the volume just cited.

From the foregoing description of the types of *Haplocanthosaurus priscus* and *H. utterbacki* it will readily appear that the affinities of that genus are with the *Morosauridæ*. The relationships with that family are shown by the expanded superior extremity of the scapula; the general form of the different pelvic elements, more especially the pubes and ischia; the simpler structure of the presacral vertebræ; the short spines of the dorsals and sacrals; the biconcave centra of the caudals and in the relative breadth and height of the sacrum. While the relationships with the *Morosauridæ* are clearly indicated by the presence of these and other characters of scarcely less importance, yet there are present certain characters even more marked than most of those which at present serve to distinguish even the most widely separated families of the *Sauropoda* now known. These are the perfectly simple neural spines of the anterior dorsals and posterior cervicals; the different position in the sacrum of the sacrals with coössified sacral spines; the greater number of dorsal vertebræ and the much simpler structure of the individual vertebræ throughout the entire vertebral column. Such differences as these will doubtless be considered by some as of family or at least subfamily importance. Since, for the most part at least, they are only such differences as we might reasonably expect to find among the more primitive and less highly specialized members of that family I prefer to regard *Haplocanthosaurus* as pertaining to the *Morosauridæ* and including species the most generalized of any yet known in that or any other family of the Sauropoda.

It is easy to see how the slight emarginations at the summit of the neural spines in the anterior dorsals and posterior cervicals of *H. utterbacki* might become successively more and more emphasized until they became actually bifid, at least to the extent that obtains in *Morosaurus*. Nor is it impossible that'while specialization was taking place along this particular direction, the centra, transverse processes, etc., may have assumed a more and more complicated structure. It is by some such process as this that the present author conceives that *Morosaurus* was developed from some earlier and more primitive form which was alike ancestral to that genus and *Haplocanthosaurus*, the latter, however, being less progressive than the former, became less modified and preserves more nearly the general form and character of their common ancestral stock.

Although representatives of both genera lived contemporaneously, as is shown by the presence of undoubted remains of both in the Canyon City quarry, it is more than probable that *Morosaurus* long survived the other since remains of that genus are abundant near the top of the Jurassic in southern Wyoming while as yet no remains of *Haplocanthosaurus* are certainly known to have been obtained there.

RELATIONS OF HAPLOCANTHOSAURUS TO EUROPEAN AND SOUTH AMERICAN FORMS.

As yet we have only discussed the relations of the present genus with North American representatives of the Sauropoda. It now remains to notice briefly the relations of this genus with certain forms from Europe and South America with which it seems to show some relationships.

Chondrosteosaurus compared with Haplocanthosaurus.

The characters exhibited by the vertebral centra of *Haplocanthosaurus* are somewhat similar to those shown in *Chondrosteosaurus gigas* Owen, founded on the centrum of an anterior dorsal or cervical vertebra from the Wealden of the Isle of Wight and described and figured in *Supplement (No. VI.) to the Monograph of the Fossil Reptilia of the Wealden and Purbeck Formations; pp. 5 to 7, Plates II–V, of Owen's British Fossil Reptiles, London, 1876.*

This resemblance is especially apparent in Plate II., Fig. 2, and Plate V., Fig. 1 of the paper just cited. However the resemblances shown are not of a character which would indicate a closer relationship between *Chondrosteosaurus* and *Haplocanthosaurus* than between the former of these with any one of several other genera of the Sauropoda. Nor is it possible, owing to the fragmentary nature of the material upon which that genus was based, to decide with certainty even as to just

what family of the Sauropoda it pertained, although Owen's statement that the
transverse diameter of the centrum exceeds the vertical together with the broad,
almost flat inferior surface and other characters indicated by the figures would seem
to fix this centrum as pertaining to a median cervical of some member of the *Morosauridæ*.

Comparison of Haplocanthosaurus with Bothriospondylus Owen.

A comparison of the various characters exhibited by the species of *Bothriospondylus* described by Owen in his Monograph on that genus published as part II., of his
Reptilia of the Mesozoic Formations, pp. 15–26, Plates III.–IX., will show many striking resemblances to *Haplocanthosaurus* and at first sight one might be led to believe
that they pertain to the same genus as that to which the material under discussion
pertains. A closer examination however will reveal several striking and important

differences certainly to be regarded as
of generic if not of family rank. Such
distinctive characters are especially ob-
servable in the sacral centra as will be
seen by a comparison of Fig. 20 showing side views respectively of the fourth
and terminal sacral centra of the type of
Haplocanthosaurus utterbacki with the
figures on Plates III. and IV., of the
monograph just cited. As will be seen
by an examination of Owen's figures and
text the median sacrals of *Bothriospondylus* are provided with both anterior and
posterior parapophysial facets, while in
Haplocanthosaurus as shown in Fig. 20,

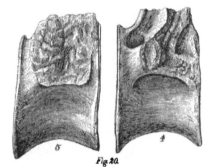

Fig 20.

FIG. 20.   4. Centrum of fourth sacral of *Haplocanthosaurus utterbacki* seen from right side (No. 879).
5. Same view of fifth or last sacral centrum of same.
Both ⅓ natural size.

there is but a single facet, which in the centrum of the fourth sacral is median in
position antero-posteriorly, but somewhat elevated above the median longitudinal
line. Furthermore the pleurocentral cavities so conspicuous in the sacral centra of
Haplocanthosaurus beneath the parapophyses are entirely wanting in *Bothriospondylus*. The cavities in the sacrals of that genus shown at *f*, Plate III., Figs. 2 and
4, and Plate IV., 4 and 5, of Owen's Monograph lie above the parapophyses and are
not homologous with the pleurocentral cavities. These characters as well as others
of only less importance are quite sufficient to distinguish *Haplocanthosaurus* from
Bothriospondylus.

Comparison of Haplocanthosaurns with Cetiosaurus Owen.

Of all the British representatives of the *Sauropoda* perhaps the most striking resemblances to *Haplocanthosaurus* are to be found in *Cetiosaurus longus* Owen, as shown in remains representing a considerable portion of a single skeleton discovered in 1868–70 in quarries of the Great Oolite of Enslow Rocks at Kirtlington Station,

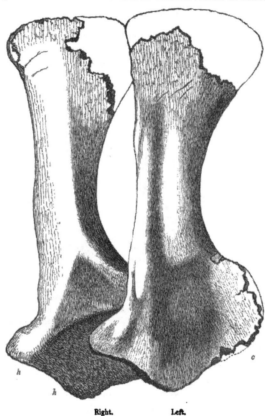

Right.   **Left.**

FIG. 21. Scapulæ of *Cetiosaurus longus* Owen, after Owen, $\frac{1}{16}$ natural size ; *hh*, surface for articulation with humerus ; *c*, surface for articulation with coracoid.

eight miles north of Oxford, and showing so close a resemblance to the type of *C. longus* that it was used by Owen in his detailed description of that species in his *Monograph on the genus Cetiosaurus in Part II. of his British Fossil Reptiles of the*

Mesozoic Formations, pp. 25-43, Plate X., text figures 1-10. The resemblances in these two forms are very numerous and are to be seen in the scapulæ, as compare Figs. 18 and 21 ; the femur, the ilium and the vertebræ as figured and described by Owen in his Monograph. Indeed, if the vertebra described as an anterior dorsal in the last paragraph on page 29 of his monograph is really an anterior dorsal this resemblance would seem to be more than superficial, for according to Owen's description the neural spine seems to be quite simple and the diapophyses are described as being directed upward and outward at an angle of 45° with the neural spine, characters precisely like those already described as obtaining in *Haplocanthosaurus*. Unfortunately Owen does not figure this vertebra, and were it not for the

fact that he describes it as being massive, one might readily believe on the evidence of this vertebra alone that it pertained to a genus closely related to or identical with those remains which I have made the type of *Haplocanthosaurus*. However the vertebræ of *Haplocanthosaurus* can by no means be considered massive when compared with the vertebræ of other members of the Sauropoda. Moreover, in *Haplocanthosaurus* the vertebræ show numerous large intra-mural cavities instead of the close, though cancellous texture of these bones, resembling that which obtains in the whales, which is present in the British genus and which suggested the generic name *Cetiosaurus*. This difference in character would seem a very important one, if it were shown to exist in those vertebræ of *Cetiosaurus* which are

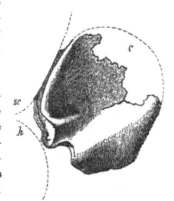

FIG. 22. Coracoid of *Cetiosaurus longus* Owen, after Owen. ⅐ natural size. *sc*, surface for scapula ; *h*, surface for humerus.

most cavernous in *Haplocanthosaurus*. There are, however, other and quite striking differences, notwithstanding the general similarity in the osteology of these two genera. The coracoid, according to Owen, is especially different, as will be apparent after a comparison of Figs. 19 and 22. If Owen's figure is correct the coracoid of Cetiosaurus is without a foramen, a character which, if correct, is entirely unique, in so far as I am aware, among not only the Sauropoda but the herbivorous dinosaurs generally. It appears to me quite possible that Owen's figure is erroneous and that the coracoid is so distorted or imperfect as not to show a foramen in the example from which his drawing was made. It does not seem possible that such a striking difference could normally have existed in the coracoids of two genera otherwise so closely related as these genera appear to be and I would suggest a reëxamination of the British specimen by those who may have access to it. While *Haplocanthosaurus* and *Cetiosaurus* are certainly generically distinct I believe they may pertain to the same family.

Although there are undoubted close similarities in structure between *Haplocanthosaurus* and the three genera of British Sauropods mentioned above, yet, if we can rely upon the characters represented by a single vertebra, it is in South America that there has been found the remains of a Sauropod dinosaur showing the closest relations with this genus. I refer to the dorsal vertebra recently described and figured by F. Baron Nopsca [8] and provisionally referred by him to *Bothriospondylus*. From Nopsca's figures, it will be seen that from the material at hand it is not generically distinguishable from *Haplocanthosaurus* the corresponding vertebra of which it resembles very closely. Note for instance the simple neural spine, elevated diapophyses, high neural arches, reduced centra, character and arrangement of the various laminæ, position and character of the tubercular and capitular rib facets, all of which are characters similar to, indeed almost identical with, those found in the median dorsals of *Haplocanthosaurus*. Without claiming that the two are undoubtedly congeneric I wish to emphasize the very striking similarity in structure which they exhibit.

From the above study of the material constituting the types of *Haplocanthosaurus priscus* and *H. utterbacki* the present author feels justified in regarding that genus as representing the least specialized member of the Sauropoda yet discovered. Of the families of Sauropoda already proposed its closest affinities are undoubtedly with the *Morosauridæ* and I prefer to include it in that family rather than to erect for it a new family, although some will doubtless think it deserving of the rank of a distinct family, the *Haplocanthosauridæ*. According to that classification of the Dinosauria which it appears to me is most acceptable, considering our present knowledge of the group, the taxonomy of *Haplocanthosaurus* would be best expressed by considering it as a well-marked genus of the family *Morosauridæ* of the order Sauropoda, subclass Dinosauria, class Reptilia.

Probable Habits of the Sauropoda.

Great diversity of opinion has been expressed by various authors regarding the habits of the different genera of Sauropod dinosaurs. Owen, on page 39 of his "Fossil Reptilia of the Great Oölite," speaks as follows of the probable habits of these

---

[8] Sitzungsberichten der kaiserl. Akademie der Wissenschaften in Wien. Mathem. naturw. Classe, Bd. CXL., Abth. 1, Feb., 1902, pp. 108–114.

giant reptiles. "These enormous *Cetiosauri* may be presumed to have been of aquatic and, most probably, of marine habits. . . ." Seeley[9] at one time considered representatives of the genus *Bothriospondylus* (*Ornithopsis*) as "*clearly ornithic*" and this idea suggested to him the name *Ornithopsis* for those reptiles.

Osborn in his memoir entitled "A Skeleton of Diplodocus" leans to the aquatic habits of these reptiles, holding that the tail is especially modified to function as a swimming organ and was provided distally with a "vertical fin"! He believes the chief function of the tail to have been that of a propeller to aid the animal in swimming and that it functioned secondarily as a balancing and supporting organ. While holding that the Sauropoda (Cetiosaurs) are aquatic and quadrupedal, he infers that they were capable of migration on land and of assuming both a bipedal and tripodal position, the tail when in the latter position functioning as a third support in conjunction with the hinder pair of legs.

Marsh was the first to advance the aquatic habits of *Diplodocus*, having considered the position of the narial opening as suggestive of such habits. In his memoir on *Diplodocus* the present author accepted an aquatic life as that to which representatives of that genus seemed best adapted when considered from their anatomical structure as a whole. I remarked in that connection "That I was inclined to the opinion that *Diplodocus* was essentially an aquatic animal, but quite capable of locomotion on land."

So similar in general form and anatomical characters are the different genera of the Sauropoda that we may consider the group as a whole as a remarkably homogeneous one, with quite similar though not identical habits characterizing most if not all of its representatives. It would seem therefore more advantageous to discuss the probable habits and mode of life of the group as a whole than those of any particular genus. In any such discussion there are several classes of facts from which evidence more or less important can be obtained bearing upon the subject. Among these may be mentioned the following:

1. *The anatomical or osteological characters of the group.*

2. *The nature of the other associated fossils including vertebrates, invertebrates and plants.*

3. *The condition in which the remains are found imbedded in the matrix.*

4. *The nature of the matrix in which the remains are found.*

Let us next consider in the order enumerated above the evidences afforded as to the life habits of the Sauropoda by these four classes of testimony.

First: As to the evidence furnished by the osteological and anatomical char-

[9] "On Ornithopsis, a gigantic animal of the Pterodactyle kind, from The Wealden." *Annals and Mag. of Nat. Hist.*, 1870, p. 279.

acters of the Sauropoda. As already observed, Marsh has considered the elevated position of the anterior nares in *Diplodocus* as evidence of an aquatic life. But this evidence, although strongly presumptive, is by no means conclusive, for there are among living terrestrial vertebrates similar conditions, more especially among the mammalia accompanied by habits which are in no sense aquatic, while such essentially aquatic or amphibious reptiles as the crocodiles, alligators and gavials have the narial opening in its normal position at the distal extremity of the snout. In like manner Owen's remark that, "These enormous *Cetiosauri* may be presumed to have been of aquatic and, most probably of marine habits, on the evidence of the coarse cancellous tissue of the long bones which show no trace of medullary cavity" is not conclusive since some of the most strictly aquatic reptilia and mammalia, as for instance the Manatee among the latter class have exceptionally dense and heavy bones. However this exception is not so important, as it might at first glance seem to be, for it is a well-known fact that in the Manatee the bones have acquired greater density and increased specific gravity in order to aid these animals in retaining a submerged position while feeding on the aquatic plants found growing on the bottom of the shallow waters in which they live. It is clear that the feeding habits of the Sauropoda required no such modification of the osseous skeleton, and that if modified at all for aquatic habits, it was in the direction of a more open and cancellous structure even than that which obtains in the Cetacea and calculated not only to give greater buoyancy to these massive quadrupeds when in water but, in addition, to give the greatest possible surface for muscular attachment compatible with the required rigidity and with the least possible weight. As Osborn, in speaking of the axial skeleton of *Diplodocus*, has truly remarked "*It is a mechanical triumph of great size, lightness and strength.*" Although the present writer cannot agree with Osborn in considering the chief function of the tail as that of a swimming organ, even in *Diplodocus* the most highly specialized member of the order, with the probable exception of *Barosaurus;* and while there seems to be no evidence whatever of the presence of a vertical fin on the tail of that genus as suggested by Osborn, I nevertheless believe that all the Sauropoda were aquatic to the extent that they frequented swamps, marshes, lakes and streams, that they were capable of swimming and that when moving about by that method the tail was a very efficient propelling organ. From the character of the modification of the chevrons of the mid- and posterior caudal regions in all the Sauropoda, however, I believe that when in a normal position, whether on land or in water, the greater portion of the tail rested on the surface of the ground, and I am not prepared to say that its function as a balancing, supporting, or defensive organ, was secondary to its function as a swimming organ. In arriving at any reasonably accurate conception of the habits and usual mode of locomotion of these dinosaurs the structure of the limbs would seem to be of the very first importance although they have not as yet been given more than a passing consideration in this connection. The limbs and feet are now pretty well known in several genera of the Sauropoda and in so far as the Jurassic forms are concerned their structure shows them all to have been strictly quadrupedal, with massive and rather long limbs and feet both behind and in front, the fore limbs with one or two possible exceptions being the shorter. In no instance yet discovered is there any marked or even noticeable tendency toward abbreviating or subordinating the limbs along the lines so universally characteristic of the aquatic or amphibious recent reptilia or mammalia. The structure of the limbs and feet in all the Sauropod genera, where those elements are known, furnish to my mind conclusive evidence that they were first of all ambulatory organs whose usual and normal functions were to give support to the body and enable the animal to walk about over the dry earth or to wade in the shallow rivers, swamps, lakes and other waters while in search of food. When engaged in the latter occupation their great size aided by their long necks would enable them to essay waters of no inconsiderable depth with little inconvenience.

Second: As to the character of the associated fossils.

Wherever remains of Sauropod dinosaurs have been found in this country, there has been found associated with them in more or less abundance the remains of Theropod and Predentate dinosaurs. The classic quarry near Canyon City, Colorado, where the types of the two species of *Haplocanthosaurus* described above were found has also yielded remains of *Diplodocus, Brontosaurus, Morosaurus,, Ceratosaurus, Allosaurus,* and *Stegosaurus*, besides other dinosaurs, crocodiles, turtles, fishes and diminutive mammals all from the immediate sandstones in which the dinosaurs occur. While in the adjacent clays there are numerous small lenticular masses of limestone abounding in fresh-water gasteropods and remains of small fresh-water plants. And in the clays themselves at a few especially favored localities the shells and casts of several species of *Unio* occur in great abundance. The character of the fauna and limited flora found associated with these dinosaurs, whether considered individually or as an assemblage is not what would be regarded as strictly aquatic. Such aquatic forms as are found like the bivalves, gasteropods, fishes, turtles and crocodiles indicate for the most part shallow waters or at least streams and lakes of only moderate extent and depth.

Third: The condition of the remains as they lay imbedded in the matrix will afford some evidence as to the habits of the Sauropoda, for it is evident that if these

ponderous reptiles were actually aquatic they would require bodies of water of no
inconsiderable dimensions and depth for their accommodation and it is not at all
reasonable to suppose that when overtaken by death either through disease, old
age or the attacks of their enemies they would seek other than their natural habitat.
Therefore if they lived and died in deep water, after death it is only natural to
suppose that their carcasses would sink to the bottom and become buried beneath
the accumulating sands and clays with the different bones of the skeleton still in
their proper positions relative to one another.   For among the strictly aquatic
forms (crocodiles, etc.) that lived contemporaneously with them there are none
sufficiently large and powerful to disarticulate the skeletons of these gigantic
dinosaurs.   Since in most instances the skeletons of these dinosaurs are found in
even more disarranged and dismembered conditions than were the two described in
the present paper it seems far more probable that, as a rule, they have met death in
or adjacent to shallow waters, or on land where their carcasses were accessible to
the terrestrial carnivorous Dinosauria, to the ravages of which the dismemberment
of the skeletons is partially due, as is sometimes evidenced by the tooth marks still
preserved on the bones: silent but unmistakable evidences of those prehistoric
feasts.

Fourth : The character of the enclosing matrix furnishes important evidence as to
the nature of the habitats of those animals whose remains it contains, especially if
considered in connection with the character of the surrounding and overlying sedimentary rocks.   If as is the case at the quarries near Canyon City, Colorado, the
bones are found imbedded in lenticular masses of coarse sandstone showing cross-
bedding it is evident that such deposits were laid down in comparatively shallow
waters.   Furthermore, if as is the case throughout the Jurassic generally, wherever
important deposits of dinosaur remains have been found, massive, coarse, or finely
bedded sandstones with or without frequent examples of cross-bedding are found
replacing the finer, more evenly bedded clays and shales both vertically and laterally even at moderately frequent intervals, it is evident that such beds were not
deposited in deep and quite waters; that the immediate region, which by every
reasonable presumption should be considered the habitat of the dinosaurs, presented
the appearance not of a great sea or lake, but rather of a flat and open country
where streams were constantly shifting their courses and the smaller lakes and
bayous, though confined within more fixed limits than the streams were not entirely
stable.   That the country was flat and open rather than mountainous is shown by
the absence for the most part, of coarse conglomerates.

Conclusions as to the Habits of the Sauropoda.

In discussing the probable habits of *Diplodocus* in his memoir on that genus, the present author remarked: "I am inclined toward the opinion that *Diplodocus* was essentially an aquatic animal, but quite capable of locomotion on land." I would now after a more thorough study of the osteological characters of several Sauropod genera in connection with more extended geological observations since conducted and bearing upon the probable physiographic features, during Jurassic times, of the regions in which Sauropod remains have been found in more or less abundance, amend this statement of my opinion as follows, making it applicable to the Sauropoda generally.

I believe: *That the Sauropoda were essentially terrestrial reptiles with amphibious habits, passing much, perhaps most, of their time in shallow waters where they were able to wade about in search of food. That their natural and normal mode of progression was ambulatory, as is abundantly evidenced by the structure of their feet and limbs, but that they were quite capable of swimming when through choice or necessity they essayed the deeper waters of the larger lakes and streams, to which they must frequently have been driven to resort for protection from their natural enemies, the contemporaneous carnivorous Theropoda with habits probably still less aquatic than were those of the Sauropoda.*

Origin of the Atlantosaurus Beds.

I have elsewhere (An. Car. Mus., Vol. I., pp. 327-341) described in some detail the geology of the country in the immediate region of the dinosaur quarries near Canyon City, Colorado. It may be of interest in this connection however to describe in greater detail some of the more important quarries of this region, rendered classic by the researches of the late Professors O. C. Marsh and E. D. Cope, and to describe the character of the various strata which in this region constitute that series of sandstones, limestones, shales and marls which together make up the 450 feet of supposedly Jurassic deposits lying between the "Red Beds" below and the Dakota sandstones above. Dr. C. A. White in his article entitled: *Fresh-Water Invertebrates of the North American Jurassic* published as Bulletin 29 of the United States Geological Survey on pages eleven and twelve speaks as follows of these deposits: "The character of the strata in which the fresh-water Jurassic fossils were found, both at the Colorado and the Wyoming localities, in addition to the character of the fossils themselves, is such as to indicate for them a lacustrine and not an estuary or a fluviatile, origin; that is the rocks are regularly stratified and have such an aspect and character as to indicate that they were deposited in one or more large bodies of water. If the strata of the Colorado and of the Wyoming localities really contain an identical fauna, it may be regarded as at least probable that they were deposited in one and the same lake. The distance between the Colorado and the Wyoming localities indicates that the supposed lake was nearly 200 miles across; and, if the Black Hills fossils also belonged to the same contemporaneous fauna, the assumed lake was much larger. The existence of a fresh-water lake of even the smaller size suggested makes it necessary to infer that there was then in that part of the North America of to-day a continental area of considerable size, for such a lake could hardly be other than a part of a large drainage system.

"But aside from these considerations, the existence of such fresh-water faunas as are represented by these collections whether in large or in small bodies of water, indicates with hardly less clearness than the proved existence of one great lake would do the synchronous existence of a large continental area. Indeed it seems necessary to assume that in the fresh waters of a large land area alone, could faunas of such a character as those which are represented by these collections be developed and perpetuated." I can fully agree with Dr. White as to the necessity of assuming the existence in Jurassic times of a continental land-mass of the dimensions intimated in his paper. But it does not seem to me at all necessary to presuppose the existence of a Jurassic lake of even the smaller or more moderate dimensions assigned by him. While I do not wish to be understood as denying the possibility of the existence of a great lake in Jurassic times extending as Dr. White has suggested from the Arkansas River in Colorado to the Black Hills of South Dakota, it does appear to me that our present knowledge of the character of the faunas, both terrestrial and aquatic (fresh-water) as well as of the lithogic and stratigraphic features exhibited by the beds themselves is decidedly against such a presumption. If I properly understand Dr. White he finds nothing in the character of the aquatic mollusca to preclude the possibility of their having lived and developed in smaller lakes. After a personal examination of the localities at Green River, Utah, at Grand River in western Colorado, Canyon City and Morrison in eastern Colorado, Como and Sheep Creek in southern Wyoming, at the Spanish Mines in eastern Wyoming, along the Big Horn Mountains in central Wyoming, about the Black Hills in South Dakota and in the country near Billings in southern Montana, in all of which localities the *Atlantosaurus beds* are exposed and exhibit in more or less abundance, the remains of those dinosaurs which are characteristic of them, I am convinced that neither the character of the vertebrate fauna nor the facts of stratigraphy at any one of these places can be taken as affording anything like conclusive evidence of the presence of a great body of water. At several of these localities, however, the occurrence at intervals of sandstones showing frequent examples of cross-bedding, ripple marks and even occasionally exhibiting footprints is conclusive proof that such sandstones had not their origin in the midst of a great lake, while the presence almost everywhere of the remains of terrestrial reptiles and less frequently of mammals tells only too plainly of an adjacent land-mass. In all this region I know of no locality where any considerable extent of the Atlantosaurus beds occurs, in which remains of quadrupedal, terrestrial dinosaurs have not been found. To my mind, this fact alone affords very strong presumptive evidence that in Jurassic times

FIG. 23. Photograph of footprint in Jurassic sandstone, near Canyon City, Colorado.

this entire region was the habitat of these dinosaurs, which it could not have been had it been covered by a great lake, for the structure of their limbs shows conclusively that the Dinosauria were not aquatic. Nor can I conceive of the possibility of the carcasses of terrestrial animals being carried out into the midst of so great a lake as that presupposed above and left in such abundance as the numbers of their bones in these deposits would indicate. An hypothesis, which it appears to me is far more reasonable and more nearly in accordance with the facts as we now know them, is to consider this region as presenting in late Jurassic and early Cretaceous times the appearance of a low and comparatively level plain, with numerous lakes, both large and small, connected by an interlacing system of river channels. The whole, when covered over with luxuriant forests and broad savannas, made possible by the supposedly tropical climate of those times, would form an ideal habitat not alone for the large Dinosauria, but for the smaller reptiles and diminutive mammals of those days and for the fishes, mollusca and other aquatic life as well.

In Figs. 23 and 24 respectively, are reproductions of photographs of a footprint from the dinosaur beds near Canyon City, Colorado, and ripple marks from the same deposits along the base of the Big Horn Mountains in Wyoming.

Fig. 24.   Photograph of ripple marks on surface of Jurassic sandstone, Big Horn Mountains, Wyoming.

In Fig. 25 there is given the reproduction of a photograph by Dr. E. H. Barbour of the locality near Canyon City, Colorado, where were located the quarries so long worked by Professors Marsh and Cope. The dark area in the middle foreground just back of the tent is the quarry so long and successfully worked by Professor Marsh and recently worked with equal success by Mr. Utterback for the Carnegie Museum. At *A* directly across the cañon and on about the same horizon was located another quarry also worked with some success by Marsh. At *B* a little above and on the same side of the small cañon, but in a slightly different horizon, in a layer of arenaceous shales there occurs a bed of Unios from which were obtained most of the species described by Dr. C. A. White as coming from this locality, while the shales underlying the thick stratum of sandstone seen at the top of the escarpment forming the cañon wall just to the left and in front of the tent contains numerous small lenses of impure limestone filled with the silicified remains of fresh-water gasteropods and the stems and seeds of small aquatic plants apparently pertaining to some species of Chara. These limestone lenses are especially abundant and quite fossiliferous at the locality marked *C* in the photograph and at a point on the same horizon of this talus-covered slope a few rods in front of the extreme foreground of the photograph and therefore not shown in the picture. The line of trees just above and in front of the Marsh quarry marks the crest of the narrow ridge that at this point separates the dry cañon in the middle of the picture from

Fig. 25. View of *Atlantosaurus beds* at entrance to Garden Park, eight miles northeast of Canyon City, Colorado. From a photograph by Dr. E. H. Barbour.

Oil Creek on the extreme left. At this point this ridge is about 100 yards in width from the brink of the cliff overlooking the bed of the creek and that of the dry cañon. In the wall facing Oil Creek at the same horizon at which the bones occur in such abundance at the adjacent quarry, dinosaur bones may be seen imbedded in similar sandstones, showing that the bone-bearing horizon extends quite through the ridge. From the great abundance in which the bones were found up to the limits of the quarry as last worked and as shown in the accompanying diagrams, it is only reasonable to suppose that many rare treasures await the explorer who has the courage and funds necessary to remove the 15 to 40 feet of sandstones and shales beneath which they now lie buried.

The isolated butte known as "Cottage Rock" seen at the head of the dry cañon in the middle background is capped with some fifty to one hundred feet of light-colored, massive sandstones generally referred to as Dakota, although neither here nor elsewhere in this region in so far as I am aware, are these sandstones clearly distinguishable from the Jurassic. Cottage Rock is situated about three quarters of a mile north of the Marsh quarry and the top of the uppermost shales in this butte which are clearly recognizable as pertaining to the *Atlantosaurus beds* is estimated to be from 300 to 350 feet above the bone-bearing horizon at the Marsh quarry.

The isolated conical butte shown in Fig. 26, and locally known as the "Nipple" is situated some 300 yards back and a little to the right of "Cottage Rock." It

FIG. 26. The "Nipple" from the north, showing in the foreground the trench cut by Professor Cope in collecting Dinosaur remains.

stands on the edge of the escarpment overlooking the valley of "Garden Park" through which flows Oil Creek. This Tepee butte is composed almost entirely of shales pertaining to the uppermost *Atlantosaurus beds*. It is capped with a mere remnant of a former sandstone ledge belonging either to the top of the *Atlantosaurus beds* or the base of the *Dakota*. About the base and over the slopes of this butte fragmentary dinosaurian remains occur in considerable abundance and the locality was worked to a considerable extent by Professor Cope. One of his abandoned trenches may be seen on the left at the foot of the butte in the photograph.

Another quarry long worked by Professor Cope is shown in Fig. 27. This quarry is situated about 500 yards west of the "Nipple" and the dinosaur bones, belonging for the most part to *Camarasaurus*, were found imbedded in a thick stratum of chocolate-colored shales immediately beneath the light-colored, heavily bedded, jointed sandstones seen at the summit in the figure and provisionally

FIG. 27. Eastern entrance to Cope quarry. Light-colored Dakota sandstone at top underlaid by chocolate-colored shales with remains of Camarasaurus.

referred to the Dakota. Between this quarry and the "Nipple" there lies a comparatively level plain some 500 yards in width covered over with a growth of juniper, piñon and other bushes characteristic of this region as shown in Fig. 28.

That quarry in this region which was perhaps worked with most success by Professor Cope or men in his employ was situated about one mile north of that last mentioned and at the same horizon, in chocolate-colored shales lying just beneath the supposed Dakota sandstones. This last quarry I have never visited, but Mr. Lucas, who was Professor Cope's principal collector in this region, accompanied Mr. Utterback to the quarry and explained to him how the bones were found. According to Mr. Lucas the more complete of the two skeletons of *Camarasaurus supremus* which are now known to have been treated as one skeleton in Cope's descriptions of the species, was found at this last locality. The location of this quarry is about one mile north of the "Nipple" and on the edge of the escarpment facing Garden Park.

The above are the most important localities that have been worked for fossils in this region although dinosaur remains have been found here at many other places but in no considerable abundance. It will be noticed from the above remarks regarding the location of the several quarries worked in this region by Professors Marsh and Cope, that the quarries operated by Marsh were in a distinctly lower horizon than those from which Cope secured his material. While Professor Cope's material all came from near the summit of the *Atlantosaurus beds*, that of Professor Marsh was derived from the lower members of those beds, certainly not more than 100 to 150 feet above the Red Sandstones. This difference in horizon, which can be represented by scarcely less than 300 to 350 feet of sandstones and shales, must of necessity represent an enormous time interval, much greater perhaps than is ordinarily represented by sedimentary deposits of an equal thickness, for from the

FIG. 28. View from near Cope quarry with the "Nipple" in the middle foreground and Cooper Mountain in the distance. Garden Park lies in a depression about 600 feet below the "Nipple" between the crest of the bluff, indicated by the line of trees on either side of the "Nipple," and Cooper Mountain.

manner in which the sandstones and shales replace one another both laterally and vertically, and from the frequent examples of cross-bedding and ripple-marked surfaces exhibited by the sandstones it is evident that the region was not one of continuous and universal deposition, but that degradation and aggradation were in simultaneous operation and that while on the whole the latter agency predominated there may have been and doubtless were considerable intervals during which erosive agencies were the more efficient of the two. As should be expected the enormous time interval which elapsed between the deposition of the sandstones of the Marsh quarry and the shales of the Cope quarries, some 350 feet higher, was sufficient to accomplish considerable changes in the dinosaurian fauna of this region, and these changes are readily apparent in the faunas from these two horizons, though for obvious reasons the present paper is not the place in which to discuss them. They will no doubt be fully recognized and discussed by Professor H. F. Osborn in his Monograph on the Sauropoda now in course of preparation for the United States Geological Survey.

Synonymy of the Atlantosaurus Beds.

Although these beds were first recognized, named and adequately described both lithologically and faunally, by Professor Marsh they have received several different appellations by subsequent authors. Scott has called them the *Como-beds*; by Cross they were referred to as the *Morrison beds*; Jenney named them the *Beulah Shales* and this name was used by Darton. Considering the usual similarity of the faunal and lithologic features of these beds wherever they are known to exist and the ease with which they may be recognized even at different and widely separated localities, it would seem somewhat unfortunate that they have received so many names.

Since Marsh's term the *Atlantosaurus beds* has priority, and has become well known through long and general usage there would seem no good reason why it should not be retained. Even should the reptilian genus *Atlantosaurus*, as contended by some but which has yet to be demonstrated, prove to be a synonym and have to be abandoned, this would not invalidate the name of the formation. It would be quite as reasonable to maintain that since Fort Union on the Missouri River from which the *Fort Union beds* took their name, is no longer in existence that this great formation should receive a new name. While the present writer is entirely in favor of basing all new formation names on geographic names taken from the localities where such formations are first studied or are best represented, it does not appear desirable to make this rule retrogressive. Such retrogressive application of this rule would not only work an injustice to many pioneers in American geology, but what is of even greater importance, it would result in augmenting still further that confusion which already exists in our geologic formation names. Surely from that standpoint alone there is sufficient reason for deprecating any attempt to duplicate such names. Nor does the plea advanced by some who have been most active in giving new names to old and well known formations, that it is easier to give a new name than to turn bibliographer and trace out the synonymy and priority of the names already given by others, give promise of being justified by the results which are sure to follow such a course. To the present writer it would appear much the better plan to accept formation names for formations already known, as we find them having due respect for priority and general usage; to adopt as a general rule for our

guidance in the conferring of new names on new formations the theory that each
such name should be derived from the name of some locality at which the formation
is well displayed and may be easily recognized and studied. It might also be well
to remember in this connection that we are no more competent to legislate for
future generations than were our forefathers.

Age of the Atlantosaurus Beds.

There has been considerable difference of opinion regarding the age of the *Atlantosaurus Beds*. By some they have been regarded as of Lower Cretaceous age and by
others as Upper Jurassic. When first discovered, these beds were referred by Professor Marsh to the Cretaceous (see *American Journal of Science*, July, 1877, pp. 87–
88). In December of this same year Professor Marsh referred these same deposits
to the Upper Jurassic and in a note describing a new fish, *Ceratodus güntheri*, from
these deposits, published in the January number of the *American Journal of Science* for 1878 he named them the *Atlantosaurus beds*. He ever after consistently
maintained their Upper Jurassic age. Cope and Hayden on the other hand referred
these beds, more especially as developed at Canyon City, Colorado, and at Morrison
to the *Dakota*, now generally recognized as pertaining to the lowermost member of
the Upper Cretaceous. The following paragraph from page 234 of the Proceedings
of the American Philosophical Society was written by Professor Cope and it is sig-
nificant in this connection. It is as follows: "Dr. Hayden visited the locality of
Mr. Lucas' excavations (near Canyon City) and informs me that the formation from
which the *Camarasaurus* was obtained is the Dakota. Professor Marsh has at-
tempted to identify what is, according to Professor Mudge, the same horizon, one
hundred miles north of Canyon City with the Wealden of England. Specimens
from the northern locality which I have examined render it certain that the horizon
is that of Mr. Lucas' excavations. Of this I may say that there is no paleontological evidence of its identity with the Wealden. The resemblance of the vertebrate
fossils to those of the English Oölite is much greater, but not sufficient as yet for
identification." Ten years later however (*American Naturalist*, May, 1887, pp. 446–
447) Cope placed these beds in the Jurassic to which they had been previously
referred by both Marsh and King and which, from the paragraph quoted above,
would seem to have been the only course open to him. Indeed there is little doubt
that when Cope first referred these beds to the Dakota he did so entirely upon the
determinations of Dr. Hayden and regardless of the paleontological evidences
afforded by the fauna they contained, which, such as it was, as is shown by the quo-
tation above, he regarded as pointing to a decidedly greater antiquity even than the

Wealden, with which Marsh had been in favor of correlating them and which was at that time very generally regarded as of Upper Jurassic age though at present considered by most geologists as representing the lowermost member of the Cretaceous.

Professor Lester F. Ward, on page 377 of Part II. of the Twentieth Annual Report of the United States Geological Survey, in commencing his treatise on the Jurassic cycads dismisses the age of these beds as developed in Wyoming with the remark that there is no doubt as to their being Jurassic, and on page 384 he says of the cycads from the Freeze Out Hills locality that "in some respects they resemble the specimens from the Purbeck beds of the Isle of Portland."

Professor Wilber C. Knight[10] has remarked as follows concerning the age of the *Atlantosaurus (Como) beds.* "There can be no mistake in assigning the Como stage to the Upper Jurassic, but it seems quite possible that it is more closely allied to the Purbeckian than to the Oxfordian."

Darton[11] is not very clear as to just what age he wishes to refer these beds. In his diagram at the top of page 387 of the paper just cited he refers them to the "Lower Cretaceous (or Jurassic)?" and immediately after on the same page in his table of the thickness of formations, and again on page 393 in describing the character and distribution of the *Atlantosaurus beds (Beulah Shales)* he refers them to the Jurassic without a query. It would seem therefore that he also favored their Jurassic age.

Osborn has I think consistently maintained the Jurassic age of these deposits. On the other hand Scott and Williston have been in favor of placing them in the Lower Cretaceous.

As already noticed Dr. C. A. White has regarded these beds as of Jurassic age though apparently relying entirely upon the evidence afforded by the vertebrates and remarking that the fresh-water invertebrates of the same beds are so modern in type as of themselves to offer no suggestion of a greater age than Tertiary. And again he adds: "Indeed so modern is the facies . . . that one is surprised to find only a single type among them which is not common among American living fresh-water species."

In discussing the age of any geological horizon which is fossiliferous two classes of evidence are of especial importance. First in importance is its stratigraphic position and second the nature of its included fossils, vertebrates, invertebrates and plants. The relative value of the different classes of fossils for purposes of correlation vary

[10] *Bull. Geol. Soc. Am.*, Vol. 11, p. 387.
[11] *Bull. Geol. Soc. Am.*, Vol. 10, pp. 387, 393.

according as the beds in question are of marine or fresh-water origin. While marine
invertebrates and most terrestrial and aquatic vertebrates are as a rule safe guides
for purposes of correlation and second only in value to direct stratigraphic evidence,
fresh-water invertebrates, plants and certain vertebrates as for instance turtles, crocodiles and some fishes are as a rule much less reliable guides.

Stratigraphic Position of the Atlantosaurus Beds.—As originally applied the term
Atlantosaurus beds refers to that series of sandstones and shales, some 450 feet in
thickness and containing the remains of dinosaurs, small mammals, etc., lying
between the red Triassic? sandstones below and the Dakota sandstones above on
either side of the cañon of Four Mile Creek (Oil Creek) near Canyon City, Colorado.
The dinosaur remains upon which Professor Marsh relied for the determination of
the age of these deposits at this locality all came from the lowermost 150 feet of the
series and it may therefore eventually prove advisable to limit the use of the term
to the lower one third of the series. Farther north in Wyoming and about the
Black Hills in South Dakota similar dinosaur beds are separated from the Red Beds
by a series of marine shales and limestones named by Marsh the *Baptanodon beds.*
These latter beds are rich in the remains of marine vertebrates and invertebrates
and are universally regarded as of Middle or Upper Jurassic age, while the overlying dinosaur beds have as universally been referred to the *Atlantosaurus beds*
usually considered, as noted above, as of Upper Jurassic age. The marine *Baptanodon beds* throughout Wyoming and South Dakota are everywhere found accompanying and underlying the fresh-water *Atlantosaurus beds* though thinning out
toward the south and entirely disappearing as we approach the Wyoming and Colorado state line. As already noticed they are entirely absent in the locality near
Canyon City, Colorado, the *Atlantosaurus beds* there resting directly upon the *Red
beds* and with at least apparent conformity. Nor does there appear to be any material break in the conditions of sedimentation in this region from the base of the
Atlantosaurus beds to the summit of the *Dakota.* If this be true it would appear
that at Canyon City the lower members of the *Atlantosaurus beds*, those worked by
Marsh and by Mr. Utterback, are the fresh-water equivalents of the marine *Baptanodon beds* farther north, while the upper beds or those worked by Cope would
become the equivalents of the *Atlantosaurus beds* at Morrison, Colorado, and at
various localities in Wyoming and South Dakota. Such evidences of stratigraphy
as there are prove conclusively that the *Atlantosaurus beds* at Canyon City overlie
the Triassic and underlie the Dakota and that they are intermediate in age between
the two and are therefore of either Jurassic or Lower Cretaceous age or that they
represent, either wholly or in part, both those horizons. The latter seems to me the

more reasonable conclusion when considered from the standpoint of stratigraphy alone.

Evidences as to Age Afforded by the Fauna and Flora.—As already noticed Professor Ward has regarded the cycads from the *Atlantosaurus beds* of the Freeze Out Hills, Wyoming, locality as indicative of a Jurassic age.

Invertebrate paleontologists have I think been unanimous in referring the marine *Baptanodon beds* to the Middle and Upper Jura. They have it appears been most frequently correlated with the Oxfordian or lower member of the Middle Oölite. By some however they have been placed in the Lower Oolite. Since, as has been shown above, there is not a little evidence in favor of considering the lowermost 150 feet of the *Atlantosaurus beds* at Canyon City as the equivalents of these marine beds in the north the age of the latter, as determined by its marine invertebrates, may be taken as having a certain bearing on that of the former series. The vertebrates of these marine beds appear to point to a somewhat greater antiquity than the invertebrates, for *Baptanodon*, the most abundant and best known form, has its nearest ally in the Liassic *Ophthalmosaurus* of Europe, and Mr. C. W. Gilmore, who is engaged in a thorough and exhaustive study of the American forms, has recently shown that the American form was not edentulous as had been supposed and that it is scarcely distinguishable, at least generically, from the European Liassic genus *Ophthalmosaurus*.

Turning now to the fauna of the *Atlantosaurus beds*, it is readily apparent that the dinosaurs offer the best, indeed almost the only reliable paleontological evidence as to their age. We have already called attention to the fact that Cope regarded the dinosaurs of the uppermost of these beds as being most like those of the English Oölite and we have shown that *Haplocanthosaurus* from the lower half of the series resembles most closely *Cetiosaurus* from the Great Oölite near Oxford.

Marsh was wont to correlate the *Atlantosaurus beds* with the Wealden which he regarded as of Upper Jurassic age. On just what evidence he relied for this correlation is not quite clear. Nor does a comparison of the dinosaurian faunas of these two horizons seem to me to warrant such correlation. While from the fragmentary nature of much of the material upon which the different genera and species are based it is clearly impossible to make satisfactory comparisons in many instances between the more closely related genera and species of American and European dinosaurs, nevertheless when comparisons of the faunas as a whole are instituted between the various American and European horizons most striking and important resemblances and dissimilarities are at once apparent. Thus while in the *Atlantosaurus beds* the Sauropoda are the predominant forms both as regards size and the number of genera, species and individuals in the Wealden they are almost entirely replaced by the Predentata and Theropoda. And the Iguanodontia so abundant in the latter formation are quite unknown in the former. The same dissimilarity though in a less striking degree is noticeable when the fauna of the *Purbeck* is compared with that of the *Atlantosaurus beds*, and it is not until we get down into the middle of the Oölite that we find a dinosaurian fuana comparable even with that of the upper and middle *Atlantosaurus beds*.

In consideration of the evidences mentioned above it appears to the present writer that the dinosaurian fauna of the *Atlantosaurus beds*, as we now know it is unmistakably Jurassic in type, but that these beds may in their uppermost members represent a portion at least of the lower Cretaceous.

CARNEGIE MUSEUM, April 15, 1903.

ADDITIONAL REMARKS ON DIPLODOCUS.

BY J. B. HATCHER.

Since publishing my memoir[1] on the osteology of *Diplodocus* additional discoveries have thrown more light on the structure of these strange reptiles. It thus becomes necessary to make certain alterations in the description and restoration then given, especially relating to the structure of the fore limbs and feet. As stated in the text of my memoir there were at that time in the collections of this museum no representatives of the fore limbs or feet of *Diplodocus* and the brief descriptions of those elements there given was based entirely upon the published descriptions by Professor Osborn and upon photographs of the limbs kindly loaned by him. Fortunate discoveries of the fore limbs and feet of *Brontosaurus* (No. 563) by Mr. C. W. Gilmore and of the greater portion of a skeleton of *Diplodocus* (No. 662) by Mr. W. H. Utterback have demonstrated two important errors in my previous paper. These are:

First.—The radial articulation at the distal end of the humerus is on the internal side and anterior to the internal portion of the ulnar articulation instead of being external and anterior to the latter as stated in my memoir. When in position the proximal end of the ulna entirely enclosed that of the radius posteriorly and

[1] *Memoirs Carnegie Museum*, Vol. I., No. 1, pp. 1-63, Pl. 1-13.

externally, as shown in Fig. 1, and its articular surface is opposed to that of the distal end of the humerus posteriorly throughout its entire breadth and presents a broad and deep anterior projection enclosing the radius externally and articulating with the anterior and external surface of the distal end of the humerus.

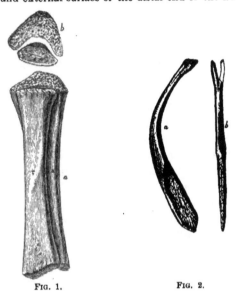

FIG. 1.   FIG. 2.

FIG. 1. *a*, front view of radius and ulna of *Diplodocus* (No. 662). *b*, proximal end of same. Both figures are one tenth natural size and show bones as seen when in position.

FIG. 2. *a*, front view of supposed clavicle of *Diplodocus*. *b*, internal view of same (No. 662), one tenth natural size.

The contact of the radius with the humerus is thus limited to the antero-internal surface instead of the antero-external as erroneously shown in my original restoration of the skeleton. The radius and ulna do not cross each other so completely as supposed by Osborn and Granger, but occupied the position relative to one another shown in Fig. 1.

Second. — The structure of the manus was entaxonic instead of mesaxonic as erroneously represented in my original restoration where, as stated in the text, I followed Osborn, having at that time no material upon which to base a restoration of those elements. The manus was doubtless somewhat more plantigrade than I at that time represented it. In the present restoration these errors in the structure of the fore limbs and manus have been corrected. The principal characters of the latter are taken from the manus of *Brontosaurus*, a detailed account of the structure of which was recently published by the writer.[2]

The Supposed Clavicles. — In my original description of *Diplodocus carnegii* I figured and described a peculiar bone which I then considered as a clavicle, though at the same time expressing some doubt as to its real nature. Fortunately we have found associated with another skeleton (No. 662) of *Diplodocus* a second and more complete clavicle? shown here in Fig. 2, *a, b*. The present specimen is somewhat incomplete at the bifid extremity, the smaller branch having been broken away, the opposite end is complete, somewhat expanded and spatulate as shown in the figures. The spatulate portion has a length of 265 millimeters, a maximum breadth of 75 millimeters and an average thickness of about 24 millimeters.

The entire length of the bone measuring along the arc of that portion of the circle which it describes is 620 millimeters. Between the expanded portion and the forked extremity the bone is irregularly elliptical or subcircular in cross-section.

This bone is asymmetrical and is to all appearances a paired bone. In neither instance have we as yet secured its opposite, though this is still possible with that one now being considered, a considerable portion of the skeleton still remaining to be unearthed. Just at the point where the rounded shaft passes into the flattened, spatulate extremity there is on one side a shallow groove running obliquely across the surface of the bone. This groove has the appearance of having been formed by the overlapping edge of a coracoid or sternal. The flattened spatulate extremity presents a slightly rugose, fibrous surface as though it had been imbedded in cartilaginous or muscular tissue, and this together with the bifid nature of the other extremity has suggested the possibility that the bone might be an os penis; in which case the bifid extremity would be the distal end and the flattened the proximal extremity. Against the probability of this assumption however, the marked asymmetry of the bone offers a potent argument and I am still strongly inclined to consider it a clavicle as which it might very readily have functioned. Although clavicles have not heretofore been recognized in the Dinosauria there would seem no good reason for supposing that they were not present in some members of that group. A clavicle of the size and form of the element under discussion, if attached to the anterior edge of the broadly expanded sternals, coracoid and prescapula, could not have failed in giving additional strength and rigidity to this portion of the skeleton.

The Anterior Cervicals. — In my former paper, owing to the incomplete nature of cervicals 3, 4, 5, they were figured as without cervical ribs; later discoveries (No. 662) demonstrate that ribs were present on all these vertebræ and they are so shown in the accompanying restoration (Plate F).

[2] See *Science*, N. S., Vol. XIV., pp. 1015–1047; and *Annals Carnegie Museum*, Vol. I., pp. 356–376.

The cervical vertebra figured by Marsh and reproduced as text Fig. 24 in my memoir on *Diplodocus*, although referred by Marsh to *Diplodocus longus*, is now known to have pertained to a species of *Brontosaurus* instead, and hence is of no value in distinguishing the different species of *Diplodocus* as I then supposed.

PLATE I.   Presacral vertebræ of type (No. 572) of *Haplocanthosaurus priscus*, one tenth natural size. Series 1, as seen from right side; Series 2, as seen from in front; Series 3, as seen from behind. *C*14 and *C*15, cervicals 14 and 15; 1, first dorsal; 6–14, dorsals six to fourteen respectively; *pzl*, postzygapophysial lamina; *ol*, oblique lamina; *hl*, horizontal lamina; *dl*, diapophysial lamina; *azl*, prezygapophysial lamina; *S*, modified surface for muscular attachment of scapula; *t* or *tf*, tubercular rib facet; *c* or *cf*, capitular rib facet, *al*, inferior blade of diapophysial lamina in first dorsal and prespinal lamina in sixth dorsal.

PLATE II.   Vertebræ of type (No. 879) of *Haplocanthosaurus utterbacki*, one tenth natural size. Series 1 and 2, dorsals; 3 and 4, cervicals; 5, anterior caudals.

PLATE III.   Nineteen anterior caudal vertebræ of type (No. 572) of *Haplocanthosaurus priscus*, one tenth natural size. Series 1, seen from right side; 2, seen from in front; 3, from behind.

PLATE IV.   1. Pelvis of *Brontosaurus excelsus* (No. 563); 2. Pelvis of *Diplodocus carnegii* (No. 94); 3. Pelvis of *Haplocanthosaurus priscus* (No. 572). All one tenth natural size and seen from left side. *il.*, ilium; *p. p.*, pubic peduncle; *i. p.*, ischial peduncle; *g. c.*, acetabulum; *pb.*, pubis; *is.*, ischium; *a.*, anterior extremity; *p.*, posterior extremity; 1, 2, 3, 4, 5, spines of first, second, third, fourth and fifth sacrals.

PLATE V.   1. Inferior view of sacrum of *Haplocanthosaurus priscus* with ilia attached (No. 572). *a*, anterior end; *p*, posterior; *pp*, pubic peduncle; *is*, ischiac peduncle; *pf*, foramen between ilium and parapophyses of first sacral.

        2. Anterior view of pelvis of same with ischia detached. *pp*, pubic peduncle; *p*, pubis; *ps*, pubic symphysis; *pt*, pubic foramen.

        3. Posterior view of same, with pubis detached and anterior expanse of ilia not shown. *ip*, ischiac peduncle; *is*, ischium. All one tenth natural size.

PLATE VI.   Restoration of *Diplodocus carnegii* Hatcher.

        From material in the collections of the Carnegie Museum, one thirtieth natural size.

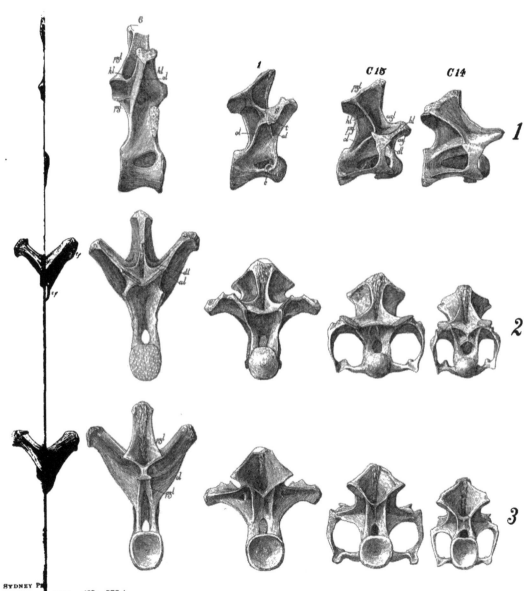

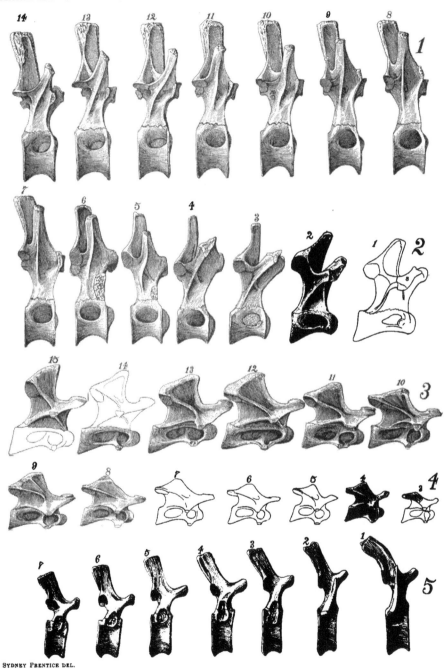

SYDNEY PRENTICE DEL.

VERTÉBRÆ OF TYPE OF *HAPLACANTHOSAURUS UTTERBACKII.* 1, 2, DORSALS ; 3, 4, CERVICALS ; 5,
CAUDALS. $\frac{1}{10}$ NAT. SIZE. (No. 879.)

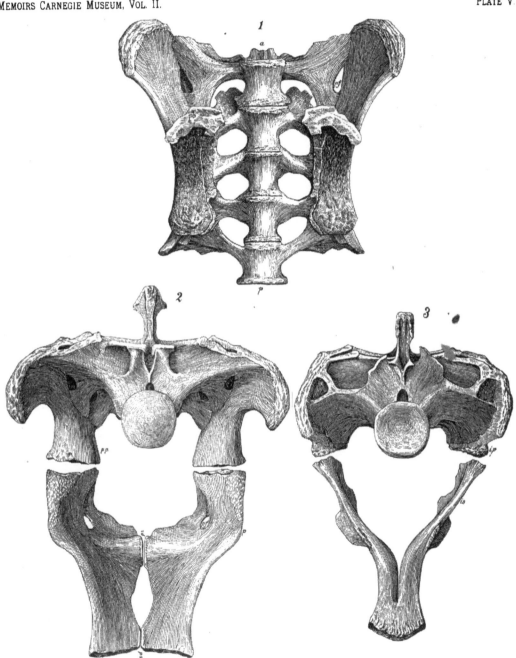

Pelvis of Type of *Haplacanthosaurus priscus.* 1, Inferior view; 2, Anterior view; 3, Posterior view.
All $\frac{1}{10}$ Nat. size. (No. 572.)

PLATE VI

Lightning Source UK Ltd.
Milton Keynes UK
UKHW031458211222
414263UK00011B/764